Wilkie Collins

New Magdalen a Novel

Wilkie Collins

New Magdalen a Novel

ISBN/EAN: 9783741161087

Manufactured in Europe, USA, Canada, Australia, Japa

Cover: Foto ©Thomas Meinert / pixelio.de

Manufactured and distributed by brebook publishing software
(www.brebook.com)

Wilkie Collins

New Magdalen a Novel

COLLECTION

OF

BRITISH AUTHORS

TAUCHNITZ EDITION.

VOL. 1325.

THE NEW MAGDALEN BY WILKIE COLLINS.

IN TWO VOLUMES.
VOL. I.

"LEAD US NOT INTO TEMPTATION."

THE
NEW MAGDALEN.

A NOVEL.

BY

WILKIE COLLINS.

COPYRIGHT EDITION.

IN TWO VOLUMES.

VOL. I.

LEIPZIG

BERNHARD TAUCHNITZ

1873.

FIRST SCENE.

The Cottage on the Frontier.

ϲ

PREAMBLE.

The place is France. .

The time is autumn, in the year eighteen hundred and seventy—the year of the war between France and Germany.

The persons are: Captain Arnault, of the French army; Surgeon Surville, of the French ambulance; Surgeon Wetzel, of the German army; Mercy Merrick, attached as nurse to the French ambulance; and Grace Roseberry, a travelling lady on her way to England.

CHAPTER I.

The two Women.

I<small>T</small> was a dark night. The rain was pouring in torrents.

Late in the evening a skirmishing party of the French, and a skirmishing party of the Germans, had met by accident, near the little village of Lagrange, close to the German frontier. In the struggle that followed, the French had (for once) got the better of the enemy. For the time, at least, a few hundreds out of the host of the invaders, had been forced back over the frontier. It was a trifling affair, occurring not long after the great German victory of Weissenburg, and the newspapers took little or no notice of it.

Captain Arnault, commanding on the French side, sat alone in one of the cottages of the village, inhabited by the miller of the district. The captain was reading, by the light of a solitary tallow candle, some intercepted despatches taken from the Germans. He had suffered the wood fire, scattered over the

large open grate, to burn low; the red embers only
faintly illuminated a part of the room. On the floor
behind him lay some of the miller's empty sacks. In
a corner opposite to him was the miller's solid walnut-
wood bed. On the walls all round him were the
miller's coloured prints, representing a happy mixture
of devotional and domestic subjects. A door of communication leading into the kitchen of the cottage had
been torn from its hinges, and used to carry the men
wounded in the skirmish from the field. They were
now comfortably laid at rest in the kitchen, under the
care of the French surgeon and the English nurse
attached to the ambulance. A piece of coarse canvas
screened the opening between the two rooms, in place
of the door. A second door, leading from the bed-
chamber into the yard, was locked; and the wooden
shutter protecting the one window of the room was
carefully barred. Sentinels, doubled in number, were
placed at all the outposts. The French commander
had neglected no precaution which could reasonably
insure for himself and for his men a quiet and comfortable night.

Still absorbed in his perusal of the despatches, and
now and then making notes of what he read by the

help of writing materials placed at his side, Captain Arnault was interrupted by the appearance of an intruder in the room. Surgeon Surville, entering from the kitchen, drew aside the canvas screen, and approached the little round table at which his superior officer was sitting.

"What is it?" said the captain sharply.

"A question to ask," replied the surgeon. "Are we safe for the night?"

"Why do you want to know?" inquired the captain, suspiciously.

The surgeon pointed to the kitchen—now the hospital devoted to the wounded men.

"The poor fellows are anxious about the next few hours," he replied. "They dread a surprise; and they ask me if there is any reasonable hope of their having one night's rest. What do you think of the chances?"

The captain shrugged his shoulders. The surgeon persisted. "Surely you ought to know?" he said.

"I know that we are in possession of the village for the present," retorted Captain Arnault, "and I know no more. Here are the papers of the enemy." He held them up, and shook them impatiently as he spoke. "They give me no information that I can rely on. For all I can tell to the contrary, the main body of the Germans, outnumbering us ten to one, may be nearer this cottage than the main body of the French. Draw your own conclusions. I have nothing more to say."

Having answered in those discouraging terms, Captain Arnault got on his feet, drew the hood of his great coat over his head, and lit a cigar at the candle.

"Where are you going?" asked the surgeon.

"To visit the outposts."

"Do you want this room for a little while?"

"Not for some hours to come. Are you thinking of moving any of your wounded men in here?"

"I was thinking of the English lady," answered the surgeon. "The kitchen is not quite the place for her. She would be more comfortable here; and the English nurse might keep her company."

Captain Arnault smiled, not very pleasantly. "They are two fine women," he said, "and Surgeon Surville is a ladies' man. Let them come in, if they are rash enough to trust themselves here with you." He checked himself on the point of going out, and looked back distrustfully at the lighted candle. "Caution the women," he said, "to limit the exercise of their curiosity to the inside of this room."

"What do you mean?"

The captain's forefinger pointed significantly to the closed window-shutter.

"Did you ever know a woman who could resist looking out of window?" he asked. "Dark as it is, sooner or later these ladies of yours will feel tempted to open that shutter. Tell them I don't want the light of the candle to betray my head-quarters to the German scouts. How is the weather? Still raining?"

"Pouring."

"So much the better. The Germans won't see us." With that consolatory remark he unlocked the door leading into the yard, and walked out.

The surgeon lifted the canvas screen, and called into the kitchen:

"Miss Merrick, have you time to take a little rest?"

"Plenty of time," answered a soft voice, with an underlying melancholy in it, plainly distinguishable though it had only spoken three words.

"Come in then," continued the surgeon, "and bring the English lady with you. Here is a quiet room, all to yourselves."   .

He held back the canvas, and the two women appeared.

The nurse led the way—tall, lithe, and graceful—attired in her uniform dress of neat black stuff, with plain linen collar and cuffs, and with the scarlet cross of the Geneva Convention embroidered on her left shoulder. Pale and sad, her expression and her manner both eloquently suggestive of suppressed suffering and sorrow, there was an innate nobility in the carriage of this woman's head, an innate grandeur in the gaze of her large grey eyes, and in the lines of her finely-proportioned face, which made her irresistibly striking and beautiful, seen under any circumstances and clad in any dress. Her companion, darker in complexion and smaller in stature, possessed attractions which were quite marked enough to account for the surgeon's polite anxiety to shelter her in the captain's room. The common consent of mankind would have declared her to be an unusually pretty woman. She wore the large grey cloak that covered her from head to foot, with a grace that lent its own attractions to a plain and even a shabby article of dress. The languor in her movements, and the uncertainty of tone in her voice as she thanked the surgeon, suggested that she was suffering from fatigue. Her dark eyes searched the dimly-lighted room timidly, and she held fast by the nurse's arm with the air of a woman whose nerves had been severely shaken by some recent alarm.

"You have one thing to remember, ladies," said the surgeon. "Beware of opening the shutter, for fear of the light being seen through the window. For the rest, we are free to make ourselves as comfortable as we can. Compose yourself, dear madam, and rely on the protection of a Frenchman who is devoted to you!" He gallantly emphasised his last words by raising the hand of the English lady to his lips. At the moment when he kissed it, the canvas screen was again drawn aside. A person in the service of the ambulance appeared, announcing that a bandage had slipped, and that one of the wounded men was to all appearance bleeding to death. The surgeon, submitting to destiny with the worst possible grace, dropped the charming Englishwoman's hand, and returned to his duties in the kitchen. The two ladies were left together in the room.

"Will you take a chair, madam?" asked the nurse.

"Don't call me 'madam,'" returned the young lady cordially. "My name is Grace Roseberry. What is your name?"

The nurse hesitated. "Not a pretty name like yours," she said, and hesitated again. "Call me 'Mercy Merrick,'" she added, after a moment's consideration.

Had she given an assumed name? Was there some unhappy celebrity attached to her own name? Miss Roseberry did not wait to ask herself those questions. "How can I thank you," she exclaimed gratefully, "for your sisterly kindness to a stranger like me?"

"I have only done my duty," said Mercy Merrick, a little coldly. "Don't speak of it."

"I must speak of it. What a situation you found me in when the French soldiers had driven the Germans away! My travelling-carriage stopped; the horses seized; I myself in a strange country at nightfall, robbed of my money and my luggage, and drenched to the skin by the pouring rain! I am indebted to you for shelter in this place—I am wearing your clothes—I should have died of the fright and

the exposure but for you. What return can I make
for such services as these?"

Mercy placed a chair for her guest near the captain's table, and seated herself at some little distance,
on an old chest in a corner of the room. "May I ask
you a question about yourself?" she said, abruptly.

Under ordinary circumstances, it was not in Grace's
character to receive the advances of a stranger unreservedly. But she and the nurse had met, in a
strange country, under those circumstances of common
peril and common trial which especially predispose
two women of the same nation to open their hearts
to one another. She answered cordially, without a
moment's hesitation.

"A hundred questions," she cried, "if you like."
She looked at the expiring fire, and at the dimly
visible figure of her companion seated in the obscurest
corner of the room. "That wretched candle hardly
gives any light," she said impatiently. "It won't last
much longer. Can't we make the place more cheerful?
Come out of your corner. Call for more wood and
more lights."

Mercy remained in her corner and shook her head.
"Candles and wood are scarce things here," she an-

swered. "We must be patient, even if we are left in the dark. Tell me," she went on, raising her quiet voice a little, "how came you to risk crossing the frontier in war time?"

Grace's voice dropped when she answered the question. Grace's momentary gaiety of manner suddenly left her.

"I had urgent reasons," she said, "for returning to England."

"Alone?" rejoined the other. "Without any one to protect you?"

Grace's head sank on her bosom. "I have left my only protector—my father—in the English burial-ground at Rome," she answered simply. "My mother died, years since, in Canada."

The shadowy figure of the nurse suddenly changed its position on the chest. She had started as the last word passed Miss Roseberry's lips.

"Do you know Canada?" asked Grace.

"Well," was the brief answer—reluctantly given, short as it was.

"Were you ever near Port Logan?"

"I once lived within a few miles of Port Logan."

"When?"

"Some time since." With those words Mercy Merrick shrank back into her corner and changed the subject. "Your relatives in England must be very anxious about you," she said.

Grace sighed. "I have no relatives in England. You can hardly imagine a person more friendless than I am. We went away from Canada, when my father's health failed, to try the climate of Italy, by the doctor's advice. His death has left me not only friendless, but poor." She paused, and took a leather letter-case from the pocket of the large grey cloak which the nurse had lent to her. "My prospects in life," she resumed, "are all contained in this little case. Here is the one treasure I contrived to conceal when I was robbed of my other things."

Mercy could just see the letter-case as Grace held it up in the deepening obscurity of the room. "Have you got money in it?" she asked.

"No; only a few family papers, and a letter from my father, introducing me to an elderly lady in England—a connection of his by marriage, whom I have never seen. The lady has consented to receive me as her companion and reader. If I don't return to England soon, some other person may get the place."

2*

"Have you no other resource?"

"None. My education has been neglected—we led a wild life in the far West. I am quite unfit to go out as a governess. I am absolutely dependent on this stranger who receives me for my father's sake." She put the letter-case back in the pocket of her cloak, and ended her little narrative as unaffectedly as she had begun it. "Mine is a sad story, is it not?" she said.

The voice of the nurse answered her suddenly and bitterly in these strange words:

"There are sadder stories than yours. There are thousands of miserable women who would ask for no greater blessing than to change places with You."

Grace started.

"What can there possibly be to envy in such a lot as mine?"

"Your unblemished character, and your prospect of being established honourably in a respectable house."

Grace turned in her chair, and looked wonderingly into the dim corner of the room.

"How strangely you say that!" she exclaimed. There was no answer; the shadowy figure on the chest never moved. Grace rose impulsively, and drawing her chair after her, approached the nurse. "Is there some romance in your life?" she asked. "Why have you sacrificed yourself to the terrible duties which I find you performing here? You interest me indescribably. Give me your hand."

Mercy shrank back, and refused the offered hand.

"Are we not friends?" Grace asked, in astonishment.

"We can never be friends."

"Why not?"

The nurse was dumb. She had shown a marked hesitation when she had mentioned her name. Remembering this, Grace openly avowed the conclusion at which she had arrived. "Should I be guessing right," she asked, "if I guessed you to be some great lady in disguise?"

Mercy laughed to herself—low and bitterly. "I a great lady!" she said contemptuously. "For heaven's sake let us talk of something else!"

Grace's curiosity was thoroughly roused. She persisted. "Once more," she whispered persuasively. "Let us be friends." She gently laid her hand as she spoke on Mercy's shoulder. Mercy roughly shook it

ROMA

off. There was a rudeness in the action which would have offended the most patient woman living. Grace drew back indignantly. "Ah!" she cried, "you are cruel."

"I am kind," answered the nurse, speaking more sternly than ever.

"Is it kind to keep me at a distance? I have told you *my* story."

The nurse's voice rose excitedly. "Don't tempt me to speak out," she said; "you will regret it."

Grace declined to accept the warning. "I have placed confidence in you," she went on. "It is ungenerous to lay me under an obligation, and then to shut me out of your confidence in return."

"You *will* have it?" said Mercy Merrick. "You *shall* have it! Sit down again." Grace's heart began to quicken its beat in expectation of the disclosure that was to come. She drew her chair closer to the chest on which the nurse was sitting. With a firm hand Mercy put the chair back to a distance from her. "Not so near me!" she said harshly.

"Why not?"

"Not so near," repeated the sternly resolute voice. "Wait till you have heard what I have to say."

Grace obeyed without a word more. There was a momentary silence. A faint flash of light leapt up from the expiring candle, and showed Mercy crouching on the chest, with her elbows on her knees, and her face hidden in her hands. The next instant the room was buried in obscurity. As the darkness fell on the two women the nurse spoke.

CHAPTER II.

Magdalen—in Modern Times.

"WHEN your mother was alive were you ever out with her after nightfall in the streets of a great city?"

In those extraordinary terms Mercy Merrick opened the confidential interview which Grace Roseberry had forced on her. Grace answered simply, "I don't understand you."

"I will put it in another way," said the nurse. Its unnatural hardness and sternness of tone passed away from her voice, and its native gentleness and sadness returned, as she made that reply. "You read the newspapers like the rest of the world," she went on; "have you ever read of your unhappy fellow creatures (the starving outcasts of the population) whom Want has betrayed to Sin?"

Still wondering, Grace answered that she had read of such things in newspapers and in books.

"Have you heard—when those starving and sinning fellow creatures happened to be women—of Refuges established to protect and reclaim them?"

The wonder in Grace's mind passed away, and a vague suspicion of something painful to come took its place. "These are extraordinary questions," she said, nervously. "What do you mean?"

"Answer me," the nurse insisted. "Have you heard of the Refuges? Have you heard of the Women?"

"Yes."

"Move your chair a little farther away from me." She paused. Her voice, without losing its steadiness, fell to its lowest tones. "*I* was once one of those women," she said quietly.

Grace sprang to her feet with a faint cry. She stood petrified—incapable of uttering a word.

"*I* have been in a Refuge," pursued the sweet sad voice of the other woman. "*I* have been in a Prison. Do you still wish to be my friend? Do you still insist on sitting close by me and taking my hand?" She waited for a reply, and no reply came. "You see you were wrong," she went on gently, "when you called me cruel—and I was right when I told you I was kind."

At that appeal, Grace composed herself, and spoke.

"I don't wish to offend you," she began coldly.

Mercy Merrick stopped her there.

"You don't offend me," she said, without the faintest note of displeasure in her tone. "I am accustomed to stand in the pillory of my own past life. I sometimes ask myself if it was all my fault. I sometimes wonder if Society had no duties towards me when I was a child selling matches in the street —when I was a hard-working girl, fainting at my needle for want of food." Her voice faltered a little for the first time as it pronounced those words; she waited a moment, and recovered herself. "It's too late to dwell on these things, now," she said resignedly. Society can subscribe to reclaim me—but Society can't take me back. You see me here in a place of trust—patiently, humbly, doing all the good I can. It doesn't matter! Here, or elsewhere, what I *am* can never alter what I *was*. For three years past, all that a sincerely penitent woman can do I have done.

It doesn't matter! Once let my past story be known, and the shadow of it covers me; the kindest people shrink."

She waited again. Would a word of sympathy come to comfort her from the other woman's lips? No! Miss Roseberry was shocked; Miss Roseberry was confused. "I am very sorry for you," was all that Miss Roseberry could say.

"Everybody is sorry for me," answered the nurse, as patiently as ever; "everybody is kind to me. But the lost place is not to be regained. I can't get back! I can't get back!" she cried, with a passionate outburst of despair—checked instantly, the moment it had escaped her. "Shall I tell you what my experience has been?" she resumed. "Will you hear the story of Magdalen—in modern times?"

Grace drew back a step; Mercy instantly understood her.

"I am going to tell you nothing that you need shrink from hearing," she said. "A lady in your position would not understand the trials and the struggles that I have passed through. My story shall begin at the Refuge. The matron sent me out to service with the character that I had honestly earned—the character of a reclaimed woman. I justified the confidence placed in me; I was a faithful servant. One day, my mistress sent for me—a kind mistress, if ever there was one yet. 'Mercy, I am sorry for you; it has come out that I took you from a Refuge; I shall lose every servant in the house; you must go.' I went back to the matron—another kind woman. She received me like a mother. 'We will try again, Mercy; don't be cast down.' I told you I had been in Canada!"

Grace began to feel interested in spite of herself. She answered with something like warmth in her tone. She returned to her chair—placed at its safe and significant distance from the chest.

The nurse went on.

"My next place was in Canada, with an officer's wife: gentlefolks who had emigrated. More kindness; and, this time, a pleasant peaceful life for me. I said to myself, 'Is the lost place regained? *Have* I got back?' My mistress died. New people came into our neighbourhood. There was a young lady among them—my master began to think of another wife. I have the misfortune (in my situation) to be what is

called a handsome woman; I rouse the curiosity of
strangers. The new people asked questions about me;
my master's answers did not satisfy them.   In a word
they found me out.   The old story again!   'Mercy, I
am very sorry; scandal is busy with you and with me;
we are innocent but there is no help for it—we must
part.'   I left the place; having gained one advantage
during my stay in Canada, which I find of use to me
here."

"What is it?"

"Our nearest neighbours were French Canadians.
I had daily practice in speaking the French language."   :—

"Did you return to London?"

"Where else could I go, without a character?"
said Mercy, sadly.   "I went back again to the matron.
Sickness had broken out in the Refuge; I made myself useful as a nurse.   One of the doctors was struck
with me—'fell in love' with me, as the phrase is.   He
would have married me.   The nurse, as an honest
woman, was bound to tell him the truth.   He never
appeared again.   The old story!   I began to be weary
of saying to myself, 'I can't get back!   I can't get
back!'   Despair got hold of me, the despair that

hardens the heart. I might have committed suicide; I might even have drifted back into my old life—but for one man."

At those last words, her voice—quiet and even through the earlier parts of her sad story—began to falter once more. She stopped; following silently the memories and associations roused in her by what she had just said. Had she forgotten the presence of another person in the room? Grace's curiosity left Grace no resource but to say a word on her side.

"Who was the man?" she asked. "How did he befriend you?"

"Befriend me? He doesn't even know that such a person as I am is in existence."

That strange answer, naturally enough, only strengthened the anxiety of Grace to hear more. "You said just now——" she began.

"I said just now that he saved me. He did save me; you shall hear how. One Sunday, our regular clergyman at the Refuge was not able to officiate. His place was taken by a stranger, quite a young man. The matron told us the stranger's name was Julian Gray. I sat in the back row of seats, under the shadow of the gallery, where I could see him without

his seeing me. His text was from the words, 'Joy
shall be in Heaven over one sinner that repenteth,
more than over ninety and nine just persons which
need no repentance.' What happier women might
have thought of his sermon I cannot say; there was
not a dry eye among us at the Refuge. As for me,
he touched my heart as no man has touched it before
or since. The hard despair melted in me at the
sound of his voice; the weary round of my life
showed its nobler side again while he spoke. From
that time I have accepted my hard lot, I have been a
patient woman. I might have been something more,
I might have been a happy woman, if I could have
prevailed on myself to speak to Julian Gray."

"What hindered you from speaking to him?"

"I was afraid."

"Afraid of what?"

"Afraid of making my hard life harder still."

A woman who could have sympathised with her
would perhaps have guessed what those words meant.
Grace was simply embarrassed by her; and Grace
failed to guess.

"I don't understand you," she said.

There was no alternative for Mercy but to own

the truth in plain words. She sighed, and said the words. "I was afraid I might interest him in my sorrows, and might set my heart on him in return."

The utter absence of any fellow-feeling with her on Grace's side expressed itself unconsciously in the plainest terms. .

"You!" she exclaimed, in a tone of blank astonishment.

The nurse rose slowly to her feet. Grace's expression of surprise told her plainly—almost brutally —that her confession had gone far enough.

"I astonish you," she said. "Ah, my young lady, you don't know what rough usage a woman's heart can bear, and still beat truly! Before I saw Julian Gray I only knew men as objects of horror to me. Let us drop the subject. The preacher at the Refuge is nothing but a remembrance now—the one welcome remembrance of my life! I have nothing more to tell you. You insisted on hearing my story—you have heard it."

"I have not heard how you found employment here," said Grace; continuing the conversation with uneasy politeness, as she best might.

Mercy crossed the room, and slowly raked together the last living embers of the fire.

"The matron has friends in France," she answered, "who are connected with the military hospitals. It was not difficult to get me the place, under those circumstances. Society can find a use for me here. My hand is as light, my words of comfort are as welcome, among those suffering wretches" (she pointed to the room in which the wounded men were lying) "as if I was the most reputable woman breathing. And if a stray shot comes my way before the war is over—well! Society will be rid of me on easy terms."

She stood looking thoughtfully into the wreck of the fire—as if she saw in it the wreck of her own life. Common humanity made it an act of necessity to say something to her. Grace considered—advanced a step towards her—stopped—and took refuge in the most trivial of all the common-place phrases which one human being can address to another.

"If there is anything I can do for you"——, she began. The sentence, halting there, was never finished. Miss Roseberry was just merciful enough towards the lost woman who had rescued and sheltered her, to feel that it was needless to say more.

The nurse lifted her noble head, and advanced slowly towards the canvas screen to return to her duties. "Miss Roseberry might have taken my hand!" she thought to herself, bitterly. No! Miss Roseberry stood there at a distance, at a loss what to say next. "What can *you* do for me?" Mercy asked, stung by the cold courtesy of her companion into a momentary outbreak of contempt. "Can you change my identity? Can you give me the name and the place of an innocent woman? If I only had your chance! If I only had your reputation and your prospects!" She laid one hand over her bosom, and controlled herself. "Stay here," she resumed, "while I go back to my work. I will see that your clothes are dried. You shall wear my clothes as short a time as possible."

With those melancholy words—touchingly, not bitterly spoken—she moved to pass into the kitchen. She had just reached the canvas screen, when Grace stopped her by a question.

"Is the weather changing?" Grace asked. "I don't hear the rain against the window."

Before Mercy could check her, she had crossed the room, and had unfastened the window shutter.

"Close the shutter!" cried Mercy. "You were warned not to open it, when we came into the room."

Grace persisted in looking out.

The moon was rising dimly in the watery sky; the rain had ceased; the friendly darkness which had hidden the French position from the German scouts was lessening every moment. In a few hours more (if nothing happened) Miss Roseberry might resume her journey. In a few hours more the morning would dawn.

Hurriedly retracing her steps, Mercy closed the shutter with her own hands. Before she could fasten it, the report of a rifle-shot reached the cottage from one of the distant posts. It was followed almost instantly by a second report, nearer and louder than the first. Mercy paused, and listened intently for the next sound.

CHAPTER III.

The German Shell.

A THIRD rifle-shot rang through the night air, close to the cottage. Grace started and drew back from the window in alarm.

"What does that firing mean?" she asked.

"Signals from the outposts," the nurse quietly replied.

"Is there any danger? Have the Germans come back?"

Surgeon Surville answered the question. He lifted the canvas screen, and looked into the room as Miss Roseberry spoke.

"The Germans are advancing on us," he said. "Their vanguard is in sight."

Grace sank on the chair near her, trembling from head to foot. Mercy advanced to the surgeon, and put the decisive question to him:

"Do we defend the position?" she inquired.

Surgeon Surville ominously shook his head.

"Impossible! We are out-numbered as usual—ten to one."

3*

The shrill roll of the French drums was heard outside.

"There is the retreat sounded!" said the surgeon. "The captain is not a man to think twice about what he does. We are left to take care of ourselves. In five minutes we must be out of this place."

A volley of rifle-shots rang out as he spoke. The German vanguard was attacking the French at the outposts. Grace caught the surgeon entreatingly by the arm. "Take me with you," she cried. "Oh, sir, I have suffered from the Germans already! Don't forsake me, if they come back!" The surgeon was equal to the occasion; he placed the hand of the pretty Englishwoman on his breast. "Fear nothing, madam," he said, looking as if he could have annihilated the whole German force with his own invincible arm. "A Frenchman's heart beats under your hand. A Frenchman's devotion protects you." Grace's head sank on his shoulder. Monsieur Surville felt that he had asserted himself; he looked round invitingly at Mercy. She, too, was an attractive woman. The Frenchman had another shoulder at *her* service. Unhappily, the room was dark—the look was lost on Mercy. She was thinking of the helpless men in the inner chamber, and she quietly recalled the surgeon to a sense of his professional duties.

"What is to become of the sick and wounded?" she asked.

Monsieur Surville shrugged one shoulder — the shoulder that was free.

"The strongest among them we can take away with us," he said. "The others must be left here. Fear nothing for yourself, dear lady. There will be a place for you in the baggage-waggon."

"And for me too?" Grace pleaded eagerly.

The surgeon's invincible arm stole round the young lady's waist, and answered mutely with a squeeze.

"Take her with you," said Mercy. "My place is with the men whom you leave behind."

Grace listened in amazement. "Think what you risk," she said, "if you stop here."

Mercy pointed to her left shoulder.

"Don't alarm yourself on my account," she answered, "the red cross will protect me."

Another roll of the drum warned the susceptible surgeon to take his place as director-general of the ambulance, without any further delay. He conducted

Grace to a chair, and placed both her hands on his heart this time, to reconcile her to the misfortune of his absence. "Wait here till I return for you," he whispered. "Fear nothing, my charming friend. Say to yourself, 'Surville is the soul of honour! Surville is devoted to me!'" He struck his breast; he again forgot the obscurity in the room, and cast one look of unutterable homage at his charming friend. "*A bientôt!*" he cried, and kissed his hand and disappeared.

As the canvas screen fell over him, the sharp report of the rifle-firing was suddenly and grandly dominated by the roar of cannon. The instant after, a shell exploded in the garden outside, within a few yards of the window.

Grace sank on her knees with a shriek of terror. Mércy—without losing her self-possession—advanced to the window, and looked out.

"The moon has risen," she said. "The Germans are shelling the village."

Grace rose, and ran to her for protection.

"Take me away!" she cried. "We shall be killed if we stay here." She stopped, looking in astonishment at the tall black figure of the nurse, standing immovably by the window. "Are you made of iron?" she exclaimed. "Will nothing frighten you?"

Mercy smiled sadly. "Why should I be afraid of losing my life?" she answered. "I have nothing worth living for."

The roar of the cannon shook the cottage for the second time. A second shell exploded in the court-yard, on the opposite side of the building.

Bewildered by the noise, panic-stricken as the danger from the shells threatened the cottage more and more nearly, Grace threw her arms round the nurse, and clung, in the abject familiarity of terror, to the woman whose hand she had shrunk from touching, not five minutes since. "Where is it safest?" she cried. "Where can I hide myself?"

"How can I tell where the next shell will fall?" Mercy answered quietly.

The steady composure of the one woman seemed to madden the other. Releasing the nurse, Grace looked wildly round for a way of escape from the cottage. Making first for the kitchen, she was driven back by the clamour and confusion attending the removal of those among the wounded who were strong enough to be placed in the waggon. A second look round showed her the door leading into the yard. She rushed to it, with a cry of relief. She had just laid her hand on the lock when the third report of cannon burst over the place.

Starting back a step, Grace lifted her hands mechanically to her ears. At the same moment, the third shell burst through the roof of the cottage, and exploded in the room, just inside the door. Mercy sprang forward, unhurt, from her place at the window. The burning fragments of the shell were already firing the dry wooden floor, and in the midst of them, dimly seen through the smoke, lay the insensible body of her companion in the room. Even at that dreadful moment the nurse's presence of mind did not fail her. Hurrying back to the place that she had just left, near which she had already noticed the miller's empty sacks lying in a heap, she seized two of them, and, throwing them on the smouldering floor, trampled out the fire. That done, she knelt by the senseless woman, and lifted her head.

Was she wounded? or dead?

Mercy raised one helpless hand, and laid her fingers on the wrist. While she was still vainly trying to feel for the beating of the pulse, Surgeon Surville (alarmed for the ladies) hurried in to inquire if any harm had been done.

Mercy called to him to approach. "I am afraid the shell has struck her," she said, yielding her place to him. "See if she is mortally wounded."

The surgeon's anxiety for his charming patient expressed itself briefly in an oath, with a prodigious emphasis laid on one of the letters in it—the letter R. "Take off her cloak," he cried, raising his hand to her neck. "Poor angel! She has turned in falling; the string is twisted round her throat."

Mercy removed the cloak. It dropped on the floor, as the surgeon lifted Grace in his arms. "Get a candle," he said impatiently; "they will give you one in the kitchen." He tried to feel the pulse: his hand trembled, the noise and confusion in the kitchen bewildered him. "Just heaven!" he exclaimed. "My emotions overpower me!" Mercy approached him with the candle. The light disclosed the frightful injury which a fragment of the shell had inflicted on the Englishwoman's head. Surgeon Surville's manner altered on the instant. The expression of anxiety left his face; its professional composure covered it suddenly like a mask. What was the object of his admiration now? An inert burden in his arms—nothing more.

The change in his face was not lost on Mercy. Her large grey eyes watched him attentively.

"Mortally wounded?" she asked.

"Don't trouble yourself to hold the light any longer," was the cool reply. "It's all over—I can do nothing for her."

"Dead?"

Surgeon Surville nodded, and shook his fist in the direction of the outposts. "Accursed Germans!" he cried, and looked down at the dead face on his arm, and shrugged his shoulders resignedly. "The fortune of war!" he said, as he lifted the body and placed it on the bed in one corner of the room. "Next time, nurse, it may be you or me. Who knows? Bah! the problem of human destiny disgusts me." He turned from the bed, and illustrated his disgust by spitting on the fragments of the exploded shell. "We must leave her there," he resumed. "She was once a charming person—she is nothing now. Come away, Miss Mercy, before it is too late."

He offered his arm to the nurse. The creaking of the baggage-waggon, starting on its journey, was heard outside, and the shrill roll of the drums was renewed in the distance. The retreat had begun.

Mercy drew aside the canvas, and saw the badly-wounded men left helpless at the mercy of the enemy, on their straw beds. She refused the offer of Surgeon Surville's arm.

"I have already told you that I shall stay here," she answered.

Monsieur Surville lifted his hands in polite remonstrance. Mercy held back the curtain, and pointed to the cottage door.

"Go," she said. "My mind is made up."

Even at that final moment the Frenchman asserted himself. He made his exit with unimpaired grace and dignity. "Madam," he said, "you are sublime!" With that parting compliment the man of gallantry—true to the last to his admiration of the sex—bowed, with his hand on his heart, and left the cottage.

Mercy dropped the canvas over the doorway. She was alone with the dead woman.

The last tramp of footsteps, the last rumbling of the waggon-wheels died away in the distance. No renewal of firing from the position occupied by the enemy disturbed the silence that followed. The Germans knew that the French were in retreat. A few minutes more and they would take possession of the abandoned village: the tumult of their approach would become audible at the cottage. In the meantime the stillness was terrible. Even the wounded wretches who were left in the kitchen waited their fate in silence.

Alone in the room, Mercy's first look was directed to the bed.

The two women had met in the confusion of the first skirmish at the close of twilight. Separated, on their arrival at the cottage, by the duties required of the nurse, they had only met again in the captain's room. The acquaintance between them had been a short one; and it had given no promise of ripening into friendship. But the fatal accident had roused Mercy's interest in the stranger. She took the candle, and approached the corpse of the woman who had been literally killed at her side.

She stood by the bed, looking down in the silence of the night at the stillness of the dead face.

It was a striking face—once seen (in life or in death), not to be forgotten afterwards. The forehead was unusually low and broad; the eyes unusually far apart; the mouth and chin remarkably small. With tender hands Mercy smoothed the dishevelled hair, and arranged the crumpled dress. "Not five minutes since," she thought to herself, "I was longing to change places with *you!*" She turned from the bed with a sigh. "I wish I could change places now!"

The silence began to oppress her. She walked slowly to the other end of the room.

The cloak on the floor—her own cloak, which she had lent to Miss Roseberry—attracted her attention as she passed it. She picked it up and brushed the dust from it, and laid it across a chair. This done, she put the light back on the table, and going to the window, listened for the first sounds of the German advance. The faint passage of the wind through some trees near at hand was the only sound that caught her ears. She turned from the window, and seated herself at the table, thinking. Was there any duty still left undone that Christian charity owed to the dead? Was there any further service that pressed for performance in the interval before the Germans appeared?

Mercy recalled the conversation that had passed between her ill-fated companion and herself. Miss

Roseberry had spoken of her object in returning to England. She had mentioned a lady—a connection by marriage, to whom she was personally a stranger —who was waiting to receive her. Some one capable of stating how the poor creature had met with her death, ought to write to her only friend. Who was to do it? There was nobody to do it but the one witness of the catastrophe now left in the cottage— Mercy herself.

She lifted the cloak from the chair on which she had placed it, and took from the pocket the leather letter-case which Grace had shown to her. The only way of discovering the address to write to in Eng-land was to open the case and examine the papers inside. Mercy opened the case—and stopped, feel-ing a strange reluctance to carry the investigation any further.

A moment's consideration satisfied her that her scruples were misplaced. If she respected the case as inviolable, the Germans would certainly not hesitate to examine it, and the Germans would hardly trouble themselves to write to England. Which were the fittest eyes to inspect the papers of the deceased lady —the eyes of men and foreigners, or the eyes of her own countrywoman? Mercy's hesitation left her. She emptied the contents of the case on the table.

That trifling action decided the whole future course of her life.

CHAPTER IV.

The Temptation.

SOME letters, tied together with a ribbon, attracted Mercy's attention first. The ink in which the addresses were written had faded with age. The letters, directed alternately to Colonel Roseberry and to the Honourable Mrs. Roseberry, contained a correspondence between the husband and wife at a time when the Colonel's military duties had obliged him to be absent from home. Mercy tied the letters up again, and passed on to the papers that lay next in order under her hand.

These consisted of a few leaves pinned together, and headed (in a woman's handwriting), "My Journal at Rome." A brief examination showed that the journal had been written by Miss Roseberry, and that it was mainly devoted to a record of the last days of her father's life.

After replacing the journal and the correspondence in the case, the one paper left on the table was a letter. The envelope—which was unclosed—bore this address: "Lady Janet Roy, Mablethorpe House, Kensington, London." Mercy took the enclosure from the open envelope. The first lines she read informed her that she had found the Colonel's letter of introduction, presenting his daughter to her protectress on her arrival in England.

Mercy read the letter through. It was described by the writer as the last effort of a dying man. Colonel Roseberry wrote affectionately of his daughter's merits, and regretfully of her neglected education— ascribing the latter to the pecuniary losses which had forced him to emigrate to Canada in the character of a poor man. Fervent expressions of gratitude followed, addressed to Lady Janet. "I owe it to you," the letter concluded, "that I am dying with my mind at ease about the future of my darling girl. To your generous protection, I commit the one treasure I have left to me on earth. Through your long lifetime you have nobly used your high rank and your great fortune as a means of doing good. I believe it will not be counted among the least of your virtues hereafter, that you comforted the last hours of an old soldier by opening your heart and your home to his friendless child."

So the letter ended. Mercy laid it down with a heavy heart. What a chance the poor girl had lost! A woman of rank and fortune waiting to receive her —a woman so merciful and so generous that the father's mind had been easy about the daughter on his death-bed—and there the daughter lay, beyond the reach of Lady Janet's kindness, beyond the need of Lady Janet's help!

The French captain's writing materials were left on the table. Mercy turned the letter over so that she might write the news of Miss Roseberry's death on the blank page at the end. She was still considering what expressions she should use, when the sound of complaining voices from the next room caught her ear. The wounded men left behind were moaning for help—the deserted soldiers were losing their fortitude at last.

She entered the kitchen. A cry of delight welcomed her appearance—the mere sight of her composed the men. From one straw bed to another she passed, with comforting words that gave them hope,

with skilled and tender hands that soothed their pain.
They kissed the hem of her black dress; they called
her their guardian angel, and the beautiful creature
moved among them, and bent over their hard pillows
her gentle compassionate face. "I will be with you
when the Germans come," she said, as she left them
to return to her unwritten letter, "Courage, my poor
fellows! You are not deserted by your nurse."

"Courage, madam!" the men replied, "and God
bless you!"

If the firing had been resumed at that moment—
if a shell had struck her dead in the act of succour-
ing the afflicted—what Christian judgment would have
hesitated to declare that there was a place for this
woman in heaven? But, if the war ended and left
her still living, where was the place for her on
earth? Where were her prospects? Where was her
home?

She returned to the letter. Instead, however, of
seating herself to write, she stood by the table, ab·
sently looking down at the morsel of paper.

A strange fancy had sprung to life in her mind
on re-entering the room; she herself smiled faintly at
the extravagance of it. What if she were to ask Lady

Janet Roy to let her supply Miss Roseberry's place? She had met with Miss Roseberry under critical circumstances: and she had done for her all that one woman could do to help another. There was in this circumstance some little claim to notice, perhaps, if Lady Janet had no other companion and reader in view. Suppose she ventured to plead her own cause —what would the noble and merciful lady do? She would write back, and say, "Send me references to your character, and I will see what can be done." Her character! Her references! Mercy laughed bitterly, and sat down to write in the fewest words all that was needed from her—a plain statement of the facts.

No! Not a line could she put on the paper. That fancy of hers was not to be dismissed at will. Her mind was perversely busy now, with an imaginary picture of the beauty of Mablethorpe House and the comfort and elegance of the life that was led there. Once more she thought of the chance which Miss Roseberry had lost. Unhappy creature! what a home would have been open to her, if the shell had only fallen on the side of the window instead of on the side of the yard!

Mercy pushed the letter away from her, and walked impatiently to and fro in the room.

The perversity in her thoughts was not to be mastered in that way. Her mind only abandoned one useless train of reflection to occupy itself with another. She was now looking by anticipation at her own future. What were her prospects (if she lived through it) when the war was over? The experience of the past delineated with pitiless fidelity the dreary scene. Go where she might, do what she might, it would end always in the same way. Curiosity and admiration excited by her beauty; inquiries made about her; the story of the past discovered; Society charitably sorry for her; Society generously subscribing for her; and still, through all the years of her life, the same result in the end—the shadow of the old disgrace surrounding her as with a pestilence; isolating her among other women; branding her, even when she had earned her pardon in the sight of God, with the mark of an indelible disgrace in the sight of man: there was the prospect! And she was only five-and-twenty last birthday; she was in the prime of her health and her strength; she might live, in the course of nature, fifty years more!

She stopped again at the bedside; she looked again at the face of the corpse.

To what end had the shell struck the woman who had some hope in her life, and spared the woman who had none? The words she had herself spoken to Grace Roseberry came back to her as she thought of it. "If I only had your chance! If I only had your reputation and your prospects!" And there was the chance wasted! there were the enviable prospects thrown away! It was almost maddening to contemplate that result, feeling her own position as she felt it. In the bitter mockery of despair, she bent over the lifeless figure, and spoke to it as if it had ears to hear her. "Oh!" she said longingly, "if you could be Mercy Merrick, and if I could be Grace Roseberry, *now!*"

The instant the words passed her lips, she started into an erect position. She stood by the bed, with her eyes staring wildly into empty space; with her brain in a flame; with her heart beating as if it would stifle her. "If you could be Mercy Merrick and if I could be Grace Roseberry, now!" In one breathless moment, the thought assumed a new development in her mind. In one breathless moment, the conviction struck her like an electric shock. *She might be Grace Roseberry if she dared!* There was absolutely nothing to stop her from presenting herself to Lady Janet Roy under Grace's name and in Grace's place!

What were the risks? Where was the weak point in the scheme?

Grace had said it herself in so many words—she and Lady Janet had never seen each other. Her friends were in Canada; her relations in England were dead. Mercy knew the place in which she had lived —the place called Port Logan—as well as she had known it herself. Mercy had only to read the manuscript journal to be able to answer any questions relating to the visit to Rome and to Colonel Roseberry's death. She had no accomplished lady to personate: Grace had spoken herself—her father's letter spoke also in the plainest terms—of her neglected education. Everything, literally everything, was in the lost woman's favour. The people with whom she had been connected in the ambulance had gone, to return no more. Her own clothes were on Miss Roseberry at that moment—marked with her own name. Miss Roseberry's clothes, marked with *her* name, were drying, at Mercy's disposal, in the next room. The way

of escape from the unendurable humiliation of her
present life, lay open before her at last. What a prospect it was! A new identity, which she might own
anywhere! a new name, which was beyond reproach! a
new past life, into which all the world might search,
and be welcome! Her colour rose, her eyes sparkled;
she had never been so irresistibly beautiful as she
looked at the moment when the new future disclosed
itself, radiant with new hope.

She waited a minute, until she could think over
her own daring project from another point of view.
Where was the harm of it? what did her conscience
say?

As to Grace, in the first place. What injury was
she doing to a woman who was dead? The question
answered itself. No injury to the woman. No injury
to her relations. Her relations were dead also.

As to Lady Janet, in the second place. If she
served her new mistress faithfully; if she filled her
new sphere honourably; if she was diligent under in-
struction, and grateful for kindness—if, in one word,
she was all that she might be and would be in the
heavenly peace and security of that new life—what
injury was she doing to Lady Janet? Once more, the

question answered itself. She might, and would, give Lady Janet cause to bless the day when she first entered the house.

She snatched up Colonel Roseberry's letter, and put it into the case with the other papers. The opportunity was before her; the chances were all in her favour; her conscience said nothing against trying the daring scheme. She decided, then and there—"I'll do it!"

Something jarred on her finer sense, something offended her better nature, as she put the case into the pocket of her dress. She had decided, and yet she was not at ease; she was not quite sure of having fairly questioned her conscience yet. What if she laid the letter-case on the table again, and waited until her excitement had all cooled down, and then put the contemplated project soberly on its trial before her own sense of right and wrong?

She thought once—and hesitated. Before she could think twice, the distant tramp of marching footsteps, and the distant clatter of horses' hoofs were wafted to her on the night air. The Germans were entering the village! In a few minutes more they would appear in the cottage; they would summon her

to give an account of herself. There was no time for
waiting until she was composed again. Which should
it be—the new life, as Grace Roseberry? or the old
life, as Mercy Merrick?

She looked for the last time at the bed. Grace's
course was run; Grace's future was at her disposal.
Her resolute nature, forced to a choice on the instant,
held by the daring alternative. She persisted in the
determination to take Grace's place.

The tramping footsteps of the Germans came
nearer and nearer. The voices of the officers were
audible, giving the words of command.

She seated herself at the table, waiting steadily for
what was to come.

The ineradicable instinct of the sex directed her
eyes to her dress, before the Germans appeared. Looking it over to see that it was in perfect order, her
eyes fell upon the red cross on her left shoulder. In
a moment it struck her that her nurse's costume might
involve her in a needless risk. It associated her with
a public position; it might lead to inquiries at a later
time, and those inquiries might betray her.

She looked round. The grey cloak which she had

lent to Grace attracted her attention. She took it up, and covered herself with it from head to foot.

The cloak was just arranged round her, when she heard the outer door thrust open, and voices speaking in a strange tongue, and arms grounded in the room behind her. Should she wait to be discovered? or should she show herself of her own accord? It was less trying to such a nature as hers to show herself than to wait. She advanced to enter the kitchen. The canvas curtain, as she stretched out her hand to it, was suddenly drawn back from the other side, and three men confronted her in the open doorway.

CHAPTER V.

The German Surgeon.

THE youngest of the three strangers—judging by features, complexion, and manner—was apparently an Englishman. He wore a military cap and military boots, but was otherwise dressed as a civilian. Next to him stood an officer in Prussian uniform, and next to the officer was the third and the oldest of the party. He also was dressed in uniform, but his appearance was far from being suggestive of the appearance of a military man. He halted on one foot, he stooped at the shoulders, and instead of a sword at his side he carried a stick in his hand. After looking sharply through a large pair of tortoise-shell spectacles, first at Mercy, then at the bed, then all round the room, he turned which a cynical composure of manner to the Prussian officer, and broke silence in these words:

"A woman ill on the bed; another woman in attendance on her, and no one else in the room. Any necessity, major, for setting a guard here?"

"No necessity," answered the major. He wheeled round on his heel and returned to the kitchen. The German surgeon advanced a little, led by his professional instinct, in the direction of the bedside. The young Englishman, whose eyes had remained riveted in admiration on Mercy, drew the canvas screen over the doorway, and respectfully addressed her in the French language.

"May I ask if I am speaking to a French lady?" he said.

"I am an Englishwoman," Mercy replied.

The surgeon heard the answer. Stopping short on his way to the bed, he pointed to the recumbent

figure on it, and said to Mercy, in good English,
spoken with a strong German accent—

"Can I be of any use there?"

His manner was ironically courteous, his harsh
voice was pitched in one sardonic monotony of tone.
Mercy took an instantaneous dislike to this hobbling,
ugly old man, staring at her rudely through his great
tortoise-shell spectacles.

"You can be of no use, sir," she said, shortly.
"The lady was killed when your troops shelled this
cottage."

The Englishman started, and looked compassionately towards the bed. The German refreshed himself with a pinch of snuff, and put another question:

"Has the body been examined by a medical man?"
he asked. Mercy ungraciously limited her reply to
the one necessary word "Yes."

The present surgeon was not a man to be daunted
by a lady's disapproval of him. He went on with his
questions.

"Who has examined the body?" he inquired next.

Mercy answered, "The doctor attached to the
French ambulance."

The German grunted in contemptuous disapproval

of all Frenchmen and all French institutions. The Englishman seized his first opportunity of addressing himself to Mercy once more.

"Is the lady a countrywoman of ours?" he asked gently.

Mercy considered before she answered him. With the object she had in view, there might be serious reasons for speaking with extreme caution when she spoke of Grace.

"I believe so," she said. "We met here by accident. I know nothing of her."

"Not even her name?" inquired the German surgeon.

Mercy's resolution was hardly equal yet to giving her own name openly as the name of Grace. She took refuge in flat denial.

"Not even her name," she repeated obstinately.

The old man stared at her more rudely than ever —considered with himself—and took the candle from the table. He hobbled back to the bed, and examined the figure laid on it in silence. The Englishman continued the conversation, no longer concealing the interest that he felt in the beautiful woman who stood before him.

"Pardon me," he said; "you are very young to be alone in war-time, in such a place as this."

The sudden outbreak of a disturbance in the kitchen relieved Mercy from any immediate necessity for answering him. She heard the voices of the wounded men raised in feeble remonstrance, and the harsh command of the foreign officers, bidding them be silent. The generous instincts of the woman instantly prevailed over every personal consideration imposed on her by the position which she had assumed. Reckless whether she betrayed herself or not as nurse in the French ambulance, she instantly drew aside the canvas to enter the kitchen. A German sentinel barred the way to her, and announced, in his own language, that no strangers were admitted. The Englishman, politely interposing, asked if she had any special object in wishing to enter the room.

"The poor Frenchmen!" she said earnestly, her heart upbraiding her for having forgotten them. "The poor wounded Frenchmen!"

The German surgeon advanced from the bedside, and took the matter up before the Englishman could say a word more.

"You have nothing to do with the wounded French-

men," he croaked, in the harshest notes of his voice.
"The wounded Frenchmen are my business, and not
yours. They are *our* prisoners, and they are being
moved to *our* ambulance. I am Ignatius Wetzel, chief
of the medical staff—and I tell you this. Hold your
tongue." He turned to the sentinel, and added in
German, "Draw the curtain again; and if the woman
persists, put her back into this room with your own
hand."

Mercy attempted to remonstrate. The Englishman
respectfully took her arm, and drew her out of the
sentinel's reach.

"It is useless to resist," he said. "The German
discipline never gives way. There is not the least
need to be uneasy about the Frenchmen. The ambulance, under Surgeon Wetzel, is admirably administered.
I answer for it, the men will be well treated." He
saw the tears in her eyes as he spoke; his admiration
for her rose higher and higher. "Kind as well as
beautiful," he thought. "What a charming creature!"

"Well!" said Ignatius Wetzel, eyeing Mercy sternly
through his spectacles. "Are you satisfied? And will
you hold your tongue?"

She yielded: it was plainly useless to persist. But

for the surgeon's resistance, her devotion to the wounded men might have stopped her on the downward way that she was going. If she could only have been absorbed again, mind and body, in her good work as a nurse, the temptation might even yet have found her strong enough to resist it. The fatal severity of the German discipline had snapped asunder the last tie that bound her to her better self. Her face hardened as she walked away proudly from Surgeon Wetzel, and took a chair.

The Englishman followed her, and reverted to the question of her present situation in the cottage.

"Don't suppose that I want to alarm you," he said. "There is, I repeat, no need to be anxious about the Frenchmen, but there is serious reason for anxiety on your own account. The action will be renewed round this village by daylight; you ought really to be in a place of safety. I am an officer in the English army —my name is Horace Holmcroft. I shall be delighted to be of use to you, and I *can* be of use, if you will let me. May I ask if you are travelling?"

Mercy gathered the cloak which concealed her nurse's dress more closely round her, and committed herself silently to her first overt act of deception. She bowed her head in the affirmative.

"Are you on your way to England?"

"Yes."

"In that case, I can pass you through the German lines, and forward you at once on your journey."

Mercy looked at him in unconcealed surprise. His strongly-felt interest in her was restrained within the strictest limits of good breeding: he was unmistakably a gentleman. Did he really mean what he had just said?

"You can pass me through the German lines?" she repeated. "You must possess extraordinary influence, sir, to be able to do that."

Mr. Horace Holmcroft smiled.

"I possess the influence that no one can resist," he answered—"the influence of the Press. I am serving here as war-correspondent of one of our great English newspapers. If I ask him, the commanding officer will grant you a pass. He is close to this cottage. What do you say?"

She summoned her resolution—not without difficulty, even now—and took him at his word.

"I gratefully accept your offer, sir."

He advanced a step towards the kitchen, and
stopped.

"It may be well to make the application as privately as possible," he said. "I shall be questioned
if I pass through that room. Is there no other way
out of the cottage?"   · .

Mercy showed him the door leading into the yard.
He bowed—and left her.

She looked furtively towards the German surgeon.
Ignatius Wetzel was again at the bed, bending over
the body, and apparently absorbed in examining the
wound which had been inflicted by the shell. Mercy's
instinctive aversion to the old man increased tenfold
now that she was left alone with him. She withdrew
uneasily to the window, and looked out at the moon-
light.

Had she committed herself to the fraud? Hardly,
yet. She had committed herself to returning to England—nothing more. There was no necessity, thus
far, which forced her to present herself at Mablethorpe
House, in Grace's place. There was still time to re-
consider her resolution—still time to write the account
of the accident, as she had proposed, and to send it
with the letter-case to Lady Janet Roy. Suppose she

finally decided on taking this course, what was to become of her when she found herself in England again? There was no alternative open, but to apply once more to her friend the Matron. There was nothing for her to do but to return to the Refuge!

The Refuge! The Matron! What past association with these two was now presenting itself uninvited, and taking the foremost place in her mind? Of whom was she now thinking, in that strange place, and at that crisis in her life? Of the man whose words had found their way to her heart, whose influence had strengthened and comforted her, in the chapel of the Refuge. One of the finest passages in his sermon had been especially devoted by Julian Gray to warning the congregation whom he addressed against the degrading influences of falsehood and deceit. The terms in which he had appealed to the miserable women round him—terms of sympathy and encouragement never addressed to them before—came back to Mercy Merrick as if she had heard them an hour since. She turned deadly pale as they now pleaded with her once more. "Oh!" she whispered to herself, as she thought of what she had purposed and planned; "what have I done? what have I done?"

5*

She turned from the window with some vague idea in her mind of following Mr. Holmcroft and calling him back. As she faced the bed again, she also confronted Ignatius Wetzel. He was just stepping forward to speak to her, with a white hand-kerchief — the handkerchief which she had lent to Grace—held up in his hand.

"I have found this in her pocket," he said. "Here is her name written on it. She must be a countrywo-man of yours." He read the letters marked on the handkerchief with some difficulty. "Her name is—Mercy Merrick."

His lips had said it—not hers! *He* had given Grace Roseberry the name.

"'Mercy Merrick' is an English name!" pursued Ignatius Wetzel, with his eyes steadily fixed on her. "Is it not so?"

The hold on her mind of the past association with Julian Gray began to relax. One present and pressing question now possessed itself of the foremost place in her thoughts. Should she correct the error into which the German had fallen? The time had come—to speak, and assert her own identity; or to be silent, and commit herself to the fraud.

Horace Holmcroft entered the room again, at the moment when Surgeon Wetzel's staring eyes were still fastened on her, waiting for her reply.

"I have not overrated my interest," he said, pointing to a little slip of paper in his hand. "Here is the pass. Have you got pen and ink? I must fill up the form."

Mercy pointed to the writing materials on the table. Horace seated himself, and dipped the pen in the ink.

"Pray don't think that I wish to intrude myself into your affairs," he said. "I am obliged to ask you one or two plain questions. What is your name?"

A sudden trembling seized her. She supported herself against the foot of the bed. Her whole future existence depended on her answer. She was incapable of uttering a word.

Ignatius Wetzel stood her friend once more. His croaking voice filled the empty gap of silence exactly at the right time. He doggedly held the hand-kerchief under her eyes. He obstinately repeated, "Mercy Merrick is an English name. Is it not so?"

Horace Holmcroft looked up from the table. "Mercy Merrick?" he said. "Who is Mercy Merrick?"

Surgeon Wetzel pointed to the corpse on the bed.

"I have found the name on the handkerchief," he said. "This lady, it seems, had not curiosity enough to look for the name of her own countrywoman." He made that mocking allusion to Mercy with a tone which was almost a tone of suspicion, and a look which was almost a look of contempt. Her quick temper instantly resented the discourtesy of which she had been made the object. The irritation of the moment — so often do the most trifling motives determine the most serious human actions — decided her on the course that she should pursue. She turned her back scornfully on the rude old man, and left him in the delusion that he had discovered the dead woman's name.

Horace returned to the business of filling up the form.

"Pardon me for pressing the question," he said. "You know what German discipline is by this time. What is your name?"

She answered him recklessly, defiantly, without fairly realising what she was doing, until it was done.

"Grace Roseberry," she said.

The words were hardly out of her mouth, before she would have given everything she possessed in the world to recall them.

"Miss?" asked Horace, smiling.

She could only answer him by bowing her head.

He wrote, "Miss Grace Roseberry"—reflected for a moment—and then added interrogatively, "Returning to her friends in England?" Her friends in England! Mercy's heart swelled: she silently replied by another sign. He wrote the words after the name, and shook the sand-box over the wet ink. "That will be enough," he said, rising and presenting the pass to Mercy; "I will see you through the lines myself, and arrange for your being sent on by the railway. Where is your luggage?"

Mercy pointed towards the front door of the building. "In a shed outside the cottage," she answered. "It is not much; I can do everything for myself if the sentinel will let me pass through the kitchen."

Horace pointed to the paper in her hand. "You can go where you like now," he said. "Shall I wait for you here, or outside?"

Mercy glanced distrustfully at Ignatius Wetzel He had resumed his endless examination of the body on the bed. If she left him alone with Mr. Holmcroft, there was no knowing what the hateful old man might not say of her. She answered, "Wait for me outside, if you please."

The sentinel drew back with a military salute, at the sight of the pass. All the French prisoners had been removed; there were not more than half-a-dozen Germans in the kitchen, and the greater part of them were asleep. Mercy took Grace Roseberry's clothes from the corner in which they had been left to dry, and made for the shed, a rough structure of wood, built out from the cottage wall. At the front door she encountered a second sentinel, and showed her pass for the second time. She spoke to this man; asking him if he understood French. He answered that he understood a little. Mercy gave him a piece of money, and said, "I am going to pack up my luggage in the shed. Be kind enough to see that nobody disturbs me." The sentinel saluted, in token that he understood. Mercy disappeared in the dark interior of the shed.

Left alone with Surgeon Wetzel, Horace noticed the strange old man still bending intently over the English lady who had been killed by the shell

"Anything remarkable," he asked, "in the manner of that poor creature's death?"

"Nothing to put in 'a newspaper," retorted the cynic, pursuing his investigations as attentively as ever.

"Interesting to a doctor—eh?" said Horace.

"Yes. Interesting to a doctor," was the gruff reply.

Horace good-humouredly accepted the hint implied in those words. He quitted the room by the door leading into the yard, and waited for the charming Englishwoman as he had been instructed, outside the cottage.

Left by himself, Ignatius Wetzel, after a first cautious look all round him, opened the upper part of Grace's dress, and laid his left hand on her heart. Taking a little steel instrument from his waistcoat pocket with the other hand, he applied it carefully to the wound—raised a morsel of the broken and depressed bone of the skull, and waited for the result. "Aha!" he cried, addressing with a terrible gaiety the senseless creature under his hands. "The Frenchman says you are dead, my dear—does he? The Frenchman is a Quack! The Frenchman is an Ass!" He

lifted his head, and called into the kitchen. "Max!"
A sleepy young German, covered with a dresser's
apron from his chin to his feet, drew the curtain, and
waited for his instructions. "Bring me my black
bag," said Ignatius Wetzel. Having given that order,
he rubbed his hands cheerfully, and shook himself
like a dog. "Now I am quite happy," croaked the
terrible old man, with his fierce eyes leering sidelong
at the bed. "My dear dead Englishwoman, I would
not have missed this meeting with you for all the
money I have in the world. Ha! you infernal French
Quack, you call it death, do you? I call it suspended
animation from pressure on the brain!"

Max appeared with the black bag.

Ignatius Wetzel selected two fearful instruments,
bright and new, and hugged them to his bosom. "My
little boys," he said tenderly, as if they were two
children; "my blessed little boys, come to work!" He
turned to the assistant. "Do you remember the battle
of Solferino, Max—and the Austrian soldier I operated
on for a wound on the head?"

The assistant's sleepy eyes opened wide; he was
evidently interested. "I remember," he said. "I held
the candle."

The master led the way to the bed.

"I am not satisfied with the result of that operation at Solferino," he said; "I have wanted to try again ever since. It's true that I saved the man's life, but I failed to give him back his reason along with it. It might have been something wrong in the operation, or it might have been something wrong in the man. Whichever it was, he will live and die, mad. Now look here, my little Max, at this dear young lady on the bed. She gives me just what I wanted; here is the case at Solferino, once more. You shall hold the candle again, my good boy; stand there, and look with all your eyes. I am going to try if I can save the life and the reason too, this time."

He tucked up the cuffs of his coat, and began the operation. As his fearful instruments touched Grace's head, the voice of the sentinel at the nearest outpost was heard, giving the word in German which permitted Mercy to take the first step on her journey to England:

"Pass the English lady!"

The operation proceeded. The voice of the sentinel at the next post was heard more faintly, in its turn:

"Pass the English lady!"

The operation ended. Ignatius Wetzel held up his hand for silence, and put his ear close to the patient's mouth.

The first trembling breath of returning life fluttered over Grace Roseberry's lips, and touched the old man's wrinkled cheek. "Aha!" he cried. "Good girl! you breathe—you live!" As he spoke, the voice of the sentinel at the final limit of the German lines (barely audible in the distance) gave the word for the last time:

"Pass the English lady!"

THE END OF THE FIRST SCENE.

SECOND SCENE.

Mablethorpe House.

PREAMBLE.

THE place is England.

The time is winter, in the year eighteen hundred and seventy.

The persons are: Julian Gray, Horace Holmcroft, Lady Janet Roy, Grace Roseberry, and Mercy Merrick.

CHAPTER VI.

Lady Janet's Companion.

———

It is a glorious winter's day. The sky is clear, the frost is hard, the ice bears for skating.

The dining-room of the ancient mansion, called Mablethorpe House, situated in the London suburb of Kensington, is famous among artists and other persons of taste for the carved wood-work, of Italian origin, which covers the walls on three sides. On the fourth side, the march of modern improvement has broken in, and has varied and brightened the scene by means of a conservatory, forming an entrance to the room, through a winter garden of rare plants and flowers. On your right hand, as you stand fronting the conservatory, the monotony of the pannelled wall is relieved by a quaintly-patterned door of old inlaid wood, leading into the library, and thence, across the great hall, to the other reception rooms of the house. A corresponding door on the left hand gives access to the billiard-room, to the smoking-room next to it, .

and to a smaller hall commanding one of the second-
ary entrances to the building. On the left side also
is the ample fire-place, surmounted by its marble
mantel-piece, carved in the profusely and confusedly
ornate style of eighty years since. To the educated
eye, the dining-room, with its modern furniture and
conservatory, its ancient walls and doors, and its lofty
mantel-piece (neither very old nor very new) presents
a startling, almost a revolutionary mixture of the
decorative workmanship of widely-differing schools.
To the ignorant eye, the one result produced is an
impression of perfect luxury and comfort, united in
the friendliest combination, and developed on the
largest scale.

The clock has just struck two. The table is spread
for luncheon.

The persons seated at the table are three in
number. First, Lady Janet Roy. Second, a young
lady who is her reader and companion. Third, a
guest staying in the house, who has already appeared
in these pages under the name of Horace Holmcroft
—attached to the German army as war-correspondent
of an English newspaper.

Lady Janet Roy needs but little introduction.

Everybody with the slightest pretension to experience in London society knows Lady Janet Roy.

Who has not heard of her old lace and her priceless rubies? Who has not admired her commanding figure, her beautifully-dressed white hair, her wonderful black eyes, which still preserve their youthful brightness, after first opening on the world seventy years since? Who has not felt the charm of her frank easily-flowing talk, her inexhaustible spirits, her good-humoured gracious sociability of manner? Where is the modern hermit who is not familiarly acquainted, by hearsay at least, with the fantastic novelty and humour of her opinions; with her generous encouragement of rising merit of any sort, in all ranks, high or low; with her charities, which know no distinction between abroad and at home; with her large indulgence, which no ingratitude can discourage and no servility pervert? Everybody has heard of the popular old lady—the childless widow of a long-forgotten lord. Everybody knows Lady Janet Roy.

But who knows the handsome young woman sitting on her right hand, playing with her luncheon instead of eating it? Nobody really knows her.

She is prettily dressed in grey poplin, trimmed

with grey velvet, and set off by a ribbon of deep red
tied in a bow at the throat. She is nearly as tall as
Lady Janet herself, and possesses a grace and beauty
of figure not always seen in women who rise above
the medium height. Judging by a certain innate
grandeur in the carriage of her head, and in the
expression of her large melancholy grey eyes, believers
in blood and breeding will be apt to guess that this
is another noble lady. Alas! she is nothing but Lady
Janet's companion and reader. Her head, crowned
with its lovely light brown hair, bends with a gentle
respect when Lady Janet speaks. Her fine firm hand
is easily and incessantly watchful to supply Lady
Janet's slightest wants. The old lady — affectionately
familiar with her — speaks to her as she might speak
to an adopted child. But the gratitude of the beautiful companion has always the same restraint in its
acknowledgment of kindness; the smile of the beautiful companion has always the same underlying sadness when it responds to Lady Janet's hearty laugh.
Is there something wrong here, under the surface? Is
she suffering in mind, or suffering in body? What
is the matter with her?

The matter with her is secret remorse. This

delicate and beautiful creature pines under the slow torment of constant self-reproach.

To the mistress of the house, and to all who inhabit it or enter it, she is known as Grace Roseberry, the orphan relative by marriage of Lady Janet Roy. To herself alone she is known as the outcast of the London streets; the inmate of the London refuge; the lost woman who has stolen her way back—after vainly trying to fight her way back—to Home and Name. There she sits in the grim shadow of her own terrible secret, disguised in another person's identity, and established in another person's place. Mercy Merrick had only to dare, and to become Grace Roseberry if she pleased. She has dared; and she has been Grace Roseberry for, nearly four months past.

At this moment, while Lady Janet is talking to Horace Holmcroft, something that has passed between them has set her thinking of the day when she took the first fatal step which committed her to the fraud.

How marvellously easy of accomplishment the act of personation had been! At first sight, Lady Janet

6 *

had yielded to the fascination of the noble and interesting face. No need to present the stolen letter;
no need to repeat the ready-made story. The old
lady had put the letter aside unopened, and had
stopped the story at the first words. "Your face is
your introduction, my dear; your father can say nothing for you which you have not already said for
yourself." There was the welcome which established
her firmly in her false identity at the outset. Thanks
to her own experience, and thanks to the "Journal"
of events at Rome, questions about her life in Canada,
and questions about Colonel Roseberry's illness, found
her ready with answers which (even if suspicion had
existed) would have disarmed suspicion on the spot.
While the true Grace was slowly and painfully winning
her way back to life on her bed in a German hospital,
the false Grace was presented to Lady Janet's friends
as the relative by marriage of the mistress of Mablethorpe House. From that time forward nothing had
happened to rouse in Mercy the faintest suspicion
that Grace Roseberry was other than a dead, and
buried, woman. So far as she now knew—so far as
anyone now knew—she might live out her life in
perfect security (if her conscience would let her),

respected, distinguished, and beloved, in the position which she had usurped.

She rose abruptly from the table. The effort of her life was to shake herself free of the remembrances which haunted her perpetually as they were haunting her now. Her memory was her worst enemy; her one refuge from it was in change of occupation and .change of scene.

"May I go into the conservatory, Lady Janet?" she asked.

"Certainly, my dear."

She bent her head to her protectress—looked for a moment, with a steady compassionate attention, at Horace Holmcroft—and, slowly crossing the room, entered the winter garden. The eyes of Horace followed her, as long as she was in view, with a curious, contradictory expression of admiration and disapproval. When she had passed out of sight, the admiration vanished, but the disapproval remained. The face of the young man contracted into a frown: he sat silent, with his fork in his hand, playing absently with the fragments on his plate.

"Take some French pie, Horace," said Lady Janet.

"No, thank you."

"Some more chicken, then?"

"No more chicken."

"Will nothing tempt you?"

"I will take some more wine, if you will allow me."

He filled his glass (for the fifth or sixth time) with claret, and emptied it sullenly at a draught. Lady Janet's bright eyes watched him with sardonic attention; Lady Janet's ready tongue spoke out as freely as usual what was passing in her mind at the time.

"The air of Kensington doesn't seem to suit you, my young friend," she said. "The longer you have been my guest, the oftener you fill your glass and empty your cigar-case. Those are bad signs in a young man. When you first came here, you arrived invalided by a wound. In your place, I should not have exposed myself to be shot, with no other object in view than describing a battle in a newspaper. I suppose tastes differ. Are you ill? Does your wound still plague you?"

"Not in the least."

"Are you out of spirits?"

Horace Holmcroft dropped his fork, rested his elbows on the table, and answered, "Awfully."

Even Lady Janet's large toleration had its limits. It embraced every human offence, except a breach of good manners. She snatched up the nearest weapon of correction at hand—a table-spoon—and rapped her young friend smartly with it on the arm that was nearest to her.

"My table is not the club table," said the old lady. "Hold up your head. Don't look at your fork —look at me. I allow nobody to be out of spirits in My house. I consider it to be a reflection on Me. If our quiet life here doesn't suit you, say so plainly, and find something else to do. There is employment to be had, I suppose—if you choose to apply for it? You needn't smile. I don't want to see your teeth— I want an answer."

Horace admitted, with all needful gravity, that there was employment to be had. The war between France and Germany, he remarked, was still going on: the newspaper had offered to employ him again in the capacity of correspondent.

"Don't speak of the newspapers and the war!"
cried Lady Janet, with a sudden explosion of anger,
which was genuine anger this time. "I detest the
newspapers! I won't allow the newspapers to enter
this house. I lay the whole blame of the blood shed
between France and Germany at their door."

Horace's eyes opened wide in amazement. The
old lady was evidently in earnest. "What can you
possibly mean?" he asked. "Are the newspapers responsible for the war?"

"Entirely responsible," answered Lady Janet.
"Why, you don't understand the age you live in!
Does anybody do anything nowadays (fighting in-
cluded), without wishing to see it in the newspapers?
I subscribe to a charity; *thou* art presented with a
testimonial; *he* preaches a sermon; *we* suffer a griev-
ance; *you* make a discovery; *they* go to church and
get married. And I, thou, he; we, you, they, all want
one and the same thing—we want to see it in the
papers. Are kings, soldiers, and diplomatists excep-
tions to the general rule of humanity? Not they! I
tell you seriously, if the newspapers of Europe had
one and all decided not to take the smallest notice in
print of the war between France and Germany, it is

my firm conviction the war would have come to an
end for want of encouragement long since. Let the
pen cease to advertise the sword, and I, for one, can
see the result. No report—no fighting."

"Your views have the merit of perfect novelty,
ma'am," said Horace. "Would you object to see them
in the newspapers?"

Lady Janet worsted her young friend with his own
weapons.

"Don't I live in the latter part of the nineteenth century?" she asked. "In the newspapers, did
you say? In large print, Horace, if you love me!"

Horace changed the subject.

"You blame me for being out of spirits," he said;
"and you seem to think it is because I am tired of
my pleasant life at Mablethorpe House. I am not in
the least tired, Lady Janet." He looked towards the
conservatory: the frown showed itself on his face once
more. "The truth is," he resumed, "I am not satisfied with Grace Roseberry."

"What has Grace done?"

"She persists in prolonging our engagement.
Nothing will persuade her to fix the day for our
marriage."

It was true! Mercy had been mad enough to listen to him, and to love him. But Mercy was not vile enough to marry him under her false character, and in her false name. Between three and four months had elapsed since Horace had been sent home from the war, wounded, and had found the beautiful Englishwoman, whom he had befriended in France, established at Mablethorpe House. Invited to become Lady Janet's guest (he had passed his holidays as a schoolboy under Lady Janet's roof)—free to spend the idle time of his convalescence from morning to night in Mercy's society—the impression originally produced on him in the French cottage soon strengthened into love. Before the month was out, Horace had declared himself, and had discovered that he spoke to willing ears. From that moment it was only a question of persisting long enough in the resolution to gain his point. The marriage engagement was ratified—most reluctantly on the lady's side —and there the further progress of Horace Holmcroft's suit came to an end. . Try as he might, he failed to persuade his betrothed wife to fix the day for the marriage. There were no obstacles in her way. She had no near relations of her own to con-

sult. As a connection of Lady Janet's by marriage,
Horace's mother and sisters were ready to receive her
with all the honours due to a new member of the
family. No pecuniary considerations made it necessary, in this case, to wait for a favourable time.
Horace was an only son; and he had succeeded to
his father's estate with an ample income to support
it. On both sides alike, there was absolutely nothing
to prevent the two young people from being married
as soon as the settlements could be drawn. And yet,
to all appearance, here was a long engagement in
prospect, with no better reason than the lady's in-
comprehensible perversity to explain the delay.

"Can you account for Grace's conduct?" asked
Lady Janet. Her manner changed as she put the
question. She looked and spoke like a person who
was perplexed and annoyed.

"I hardly like to own it," Horace answered, "but
I am afraid she has some motive for deferring our
marriage, which she cannot confide either to you or
to me."

Lady Janet started.

"What makes you think that?" she asked.

"I have once or twice caught her in tears. Every

now and then—sometimes when she is talking quite gaily—she suddenly changes colour, and becomes silent and depressed. Just now, when she left the table (didn't you notice it?), she looked at me in the strangest way—almost as if she was sorry for me. What do these things mean?"

Horace's reply, instead of increasing Lady Janet's anxiety, seemed to relieve it. He had observed nothing which she had not noticed herself. "You foolish boy!" she said, "the meaning is plain enough. Grace has been out of health for some time past. The doctor recommends change of air. I shall take her away with me."

'It would be more to the purpose," Horace rejoined, "if *I* took her away with me. She might consent, if you would only use your influence. Is it asking too much to ask you to persuade her? My mother and my sisters have written to her, and have produced no effect. Do me the greatest of all kindnesses—speak to her to-day!" He paused; and, possessing himself of Lady Janet's hand, pressed it entreatingly. "You have always been so good to me," he said softly, and pressed it again.

The old lady looked at him. It was impossible

to dispute that there were attractions in Horace Holmcroft's face which made it well worth looking at.
Many a woman might have envied him his clear complexion, his bright blue eyes, and the warm amber
tint in his light Saxon hair. Men—especially men
skilled in observing physiognomy—might have noticed
in the shape of his forehead, and in the line of his
upper lip, the signs indicative of a moral nature de-
ficient in largeness and breadth—of a mind easily
accessible to strong prejudices, and obstinate in
maintaining those prejudices in the face of conviction
itself. To the observation of women, these remote
defects were too far below the surface to be visible.
He charmed the sex in general by his rare personal ad-
vantages; and by the graceful deference of his manner.
To Lady Janet he was endeared, not by his own
merits only, but by old associations that were connected with him. His father had been one of her
many admirers in her young days. Circumstances
had parted them. Her marriage to another man had
been a childless marriage. In past times, when the
boy Horace had come to her from school, she had
cherished a secret fancy (too absurd to be communicated to any living creature) that he ought to

have been *her* son, and might have been her son, if she had married his father! She smiled charmingly, old as she was—she yielded as his mother might have yielded—when the young man took her hand, and entreated her to interest herself in his marriage. "Must I really speak to Grace?" she asked, with a gentleness of tone and manner far from characteristic, on ordinary occasions, of the lady of Mablethorpe House. Horace saw that he had gained his point. He sprang to his feet; his eyes turned eagerly in the direction of the conservatory; his handsome face was radiant with hope. Lady Janet (with her mind full of his father) stole a last look at him—sighed as she thought of the vanished days—and recovered herself.

"Go to the smoking-room," she said, giving him a push towards the door. "Away with you, and cultivate the favourite vice of the nineteenth century." Horace attempted to express his gratitude. "Go and smoke!" was all she said, pushing him out. "Go and smoke!"

Left by herself, Lady Janet took a turn in the room, and considered a little.

Horace's discontent was not unreasonable. There was really no excuse for the delay of which he complained. Whether the young lady had a special motive for hanging back, or whether she was merely fretting beçause she did not know her own mind, it was, in either case, necessary to come to a distinct understanding, sooner or later, on the serious question of the marriage. The difficulty was, how to approach the subject without giving offence. "I don't understand the young women of the present generation," thought Lady Janet. "In my time, when we were fond of a man, we were ready to marry him at a moment's notice. And this is an age of progress! They ought to be readier still."

Arriving, by her own process of induction, at this inevitable conclusion, she decided to try what her influence could accomplish, and to trust to the inspiration of the moment for exerting it in the right way. "Grace!" she called out, approaching the conservatory door.

The tall lithe figure in its grey dress glided into view, and stood relieved against the green background of the winter-garden.

"Did your ladyship call me?"

"Yes; I want to speak to you. Come and sit down by me."

With those words, Lady Janet led the way to a sofa, and placed her companion by her side.

———

CHAPTER VII.

The Man is coming.

"You look very pale this morning, my child."

Mercy sighed wearily. "I am not well," she answered. "The slightest noises startle me. I feel tired if I only walk across the room."

Lady Janet patted her kindly on the shoulder. "We must try what a change will do for you. Which shall it be? the Continent, or the sea-side?"

"Your ladyship is too kind to me."

"It is impossible to be too kind to you."

Mercy started. The colour flowed charmingly over her pale face. "Oh!" she exclaimed impulsively. "Say that again!"

"Say it again?" repeated Lady Janet, with a look of surprise.

"Yes! Don't think me presuming; only think me vain. I can't hear you say too often that you have learnt to like me. Is it really a pleasure to you to have me in the house? Have I always behaved well since I have been with you?"

(The one excuse for the act of personation—if excuse there could be—lay in the affirmative answer to those questions. It would be something, surely, to say of the false Grace that the true Grace could not have been worthier of her welcome, if the true Grace had been received at Mablethorpe House!)

Lady Janet was partly touched, partly amused, by the extraordinary earnestness of the appeal that had been made to her.

"Have you behaved well?" she repeated. "My dear, you talk as if you were a child!" She laid her hand caressingly on Mercy's arm, and continued, in a graver tone: "It is hardly too much to say, Grace, that I bless the day when you first came to me. I do believe I could be hardly fonder of you if you were my own daughter."

Mercy suddenly turned her head aside, so as to hide her face. Lady Janet, still touching her arm, felt it tremble. "What is the matter with you?" she asked, in her abrupt, downright manner.

"I am only very grateful to your ladyship—that is all."

The words were spoken faintly, in broken tones. The face was still averted from Lady Janet's view.

"What have I said to provoke this?" wondered the old lady. "Is she in the melting mood to-day? If she is, now is the time to say a word for Horace!" Keeping that excellent object in view, Lady Janet approached the delicate topic with all needful caution at starting.

"We have got on so well together," she resumed, "that it will not be easy for either of us to feel reconciled to a change in our lives. At my age, it will fall hardest on me. What shall I do, Grace, when the day comes for parting with my adopted daughter?"

Mercy started, and showed her face again. The traces of tears were in her eyes. "Why should I leave you?" she asked, in a tone of alarm.

"Surely you know!" exclaimed Lady Janet.

"Indeed I don't. Tell me why."

"Ask Horace to tell you."

The last allusion was too plain to be misunderstood. Mercy's head drooped. She began to tremble again. Lady Janet looked at her in blank amazement.

"Is there anything wrong between Horace and you?" she asked.

"No."

"You know your own heart, my dear child? You have surely not encouraged Horace, without loving him?"

"Oh, no!"

"And yet——"

For the first time in their experience of each other, Mercy ventured to interrupt her benefactress. "Dear Lady Janet," she interposed, gently, "I am in no hurry to be married. There will be plenty of time in the future to talk of that. You had something you wished to say to me. What is it?"

It was no easy matter to disconcert Lady Janet Roy. But that last question fairly reduced her to silence. After all that had passed, there sat her young companion, innocent of the faintest suspicion of the subject that was to be discussed between them! "What are the young women of the present time made of?" thought the old lady, utterly at a loss to know what to say next. Mercy waited, on her side, with an impenetrable patience which only aggravated the difficulties of the position. The silence was fast threatening to bring the interview to a sudden and untimely end—when the door from the library opened, and a man-servant, bearing a little silver salver, entered the room.

Lady Janet's rising sense of annoyance instantly seized on the servant as a victim. "What do you want?" she asked, sharply. "I never rang for you."

"A letter, my lady. The messenger waits for an answer."

The man presented his salver, with the letter on it, and withdrew.

Lady Janet recognised the handwriting on the address with a look of surprise. "Excuse me, my dear," she said, pausing, with her old-fashioned courtesy, before she opened the envelope. Mercy made the necessary acknowledgment, and moved away to the other end of the room; little thinking that the arrival of the letter marked a crisis in her life. Lady Janet put on her spectacles. "Odd, that he should have come back already!" she said to herself, as she threw the empty envelope on the table.

The letter contained these lines; the writer of them being no other than the man who had preached in the chapel of the Refuge: —

"DEAR AUNT,

"I am back again in London, before my time. My friend the rector has shortened his holiday, and has resumed his duties in the country. I am afraid you will blame me when you hear of the reasons which have hastened his return. The sooner I make my confession, the easier I shall feel. Besides, I have a special object in wishing to see you as soon as possible. May I follow my letter to Mablethorpe House? And may I present a lady to you—a perfect stranger —in whom I am interested? Pray say Yes, by the bearer, and oblige your affectionate nephew,

"JULIAN GRAY."

Lady Janet referred again suspiciously to the sentence in the letter which alluded to the "lady."

Julian Gray was her only surviving nephew, the son of a favourite sister whom she had lost. He would have held no very exalted position in the estimation of his aunt—who regarded his views in politics and religion with the strongest aversion—but for his marked resemblance to his mother. This pleaded for him with the old lady; aided, as it was, by the pride that she secretly felt in the early celebrity

which the young clergyman had achieved as a writer
and a preacher. Thanks to these mitigating circumstances, and to Julian's inexhaustible good humour,
the aunt and the nephew generally met on friendly
terms. Apart from what she called "his detestable
opinions," Lady Janet was sufficiently interested in
Julian to feel some curiosity about the mysterious
"lady" mentioned in the letter. Had he determined
to settle in life? Was his choice already made? And
if so, would it prove to be a choice acceptable to the
family? Lady Janet's bright face showed signs of
doubt as she asked herself that last question. Julian's
liberal views were capable of leading him to danger-
ous extremes. His aunt shook her head ominously as
she rose from the sofa, and advanced to the library
door.

"Grace," she said, pausing and turning round, "I
have a note to write to my nephew. I shall be back
directly."

Mercy approached her, from the opposite extremity
of the room, with an exclamation of surprise.

"Your nephew?" she repeated. "Your ladyship
never told me you had a nephew."

Lady Janet laughed. "I must have had it on the

tip of my tongue to tell you, over and over again,"
she said. "But we have had so many things to talk
about—and, to own the truth, my nephew is not one
of my favourite subjects of conversation. I don't mean
that I dislike him; I detest his principles, my dear,
that's all. However, you shall form your own opinion
of him; he is coming to see me to-day. Wait here
till I return; I have something more to say about
Horace."

Mercy opened the library door for her, closed it
again, and walked slowly to and fro alone in the
room, thinking.

Was her mind running on Lady Janet's nephew?
No. Lady Janet's brief allusion to her relative had
not led her into alluding to him by his name. Mercy
was still as ignorant as ever that the preacher at the
Refuge and the nephew of her benefactress were one
and the same man. Her memory was busy, now, with
the tribute which Lady Janet had paid to her at the
outset of the interview between them: "It is hardly
too much to say, Grace, that I bless the day when
you first came to me." For the moment, there was
balm for her wounded spirit in the remembrance of
those words. Grace Roseberry herself could surely

have earned no sweeter praise than the praise that she
had won. The next instant she was seized with a
sudden horror of her own successful fraud. The
sense of her degradation had never been so bitterly
present to her as at that moment. If she could only
confess the truth—if she could innocently enjoy her
harmless life at Mablethorpe House—what a grateful,
happy woman she might be! Was it possible (if she
made the confession) to trust to her own good conduct to plead her excuse? No! Her calmer sense
warned her that it was hopeless. The place she had
won—honestly won—in Lady Janet's estimation, had
been obtained by a trick. Nothing could alter, nothing could excuse *that*. She took out her handkerchief, and dashed away the useless tears that had
gathered in her eyes, and tried to turn her thoughts
some other way. What was it Lady Janet had said
on going into the library? She had said she was
coming back to speak about Horace. Mercy guessed
what the object was; she knew but too well what
Horace wanted of her. How was she to meet the
emergency? In the name of Heaven what was to be
done? Could she let the man who loved her—the
man whom *she* loved—drift blindfold into marriage

with such a woman as she had been? No! it was her duty to warn him. How? Could she break his heart, could she lay his life waste, by speaking the cruel words which might part them for ever? "I can't tell him! I won't tell him!" she burst out passionately. "The disgrace of it would kill me!" Her varying mood changed as the words escaped her. A reckless defiance of her own better nature—that saddest of all the forms in which a woman's misery can express itself—filled her heart with its poisoning bitterness. She sat down again on the sofa, with eyes that glittered, and cheeks suffused with an angry red. "I am no worse than another woman!" she thought. "Another woman might have married him for his money." The next moment the miserable insufficiency of her own excuse for deceiving him showed its hollowness, self-exposed. She covered her face with her hands, and found refuge—where she had often found refuge before—in the helpless resignation of despair. "Oh, that I had died before I entered this house! Oh, that I could die and have done with it, at this moment!" So the struggle had ended with her hundreds of times already. So it ended now.

The door leading into the billiard-room opened softly. Horace Holmcroft had waited to hear the result of Lady Janet's interference in his favour, until he could wait no longer.

He looked in cautiously; ready to withdraw again unnoticed, if the two were still talking together. The absence of Lady Janet suggested that the interview had come to an end. Was his betrothed wife waiting alone to speak to him on his return to the room? He advanced a few steps. She never moved—she sat heedless, absorbed in her thoughts. Were they thoughts of *him?* He advanced a little nearer, and called to her.

"Grace!"

She sprang to her feet, with a faint cry. "I wish you wouldn't startle me," she said, irritably, sinking back on the sofa. "Any sudden alarm sets my heart beating as if it would choke me."

Horace pleaded for pardon with a lover's humility. In her present state of nervous irritation, she was not to be appeased. She looked away from him in silence. Entirely ignorant of the paroxysm of mental suffering through which she had just passed, he seated himself by her side, and asked her gently if she had seen

Lady Janet. She made an affirmative answer with an unreasonable impatience of tone and manner which would have warned an older and more experienced man to give her time before he spoke again. Horace was young, and weary of the suspense that he had endured in the other room. He unwisely pressed her with another question.

"Has Lady Janet mentioned my name in speaking to you?"

She turned on him angrily before he could add a word more. "You have tried to make her hurry me into marrying you," she burst out. "I see it in your face!"

Plain as the warning was this time, Horace still failed to interpret it in the right way. "Don't be angry!" he said, good-humouredly. "Is it so very inexcusable to ask Lady Janet to intercede for me? *I* have tried to persuade you in vain. My mother and my sisters have pleaded for me, and you turn a deaf ear ——"

She could endure it no longer. She stamped her foot on the floor with hysterical vehemence. "I am weary of hearing of your mother and your sisters!" she broke in violently. "You talk of nothing else."

It was just possible to make one more mistake in dealing with her — and Horace made it. He took offence on his side, and rose from the sofa. His mother and sisters were high authorities in his estimation; they variously represented his ideal of perfection in women. He withdrew to the opposite extremity of the room, and administered the severest reproof that he could think of on the spur of the moment.

"It would be well, Grace, if you followed the example set you by my mother and my sisters," he said. "*They* are not in the habit of speaking cruelly to those who love them."

To all appearance, the rebuke failed to produce the slightest effect. She seemed to be as indifferent to it as if it had not reached her ears. There was a spirit in her—a miserable spirit, born of her own bitter experience—which rose in revolt against Horace's habitual glorification of the ladies of his family. "It sickens me," she thought to herself, "to hear of the virtues of women who have never been tempted! Where is the merit of living reputably when your life is one course of prosperity and enjoyment? Has his mother known starvation? Have his sisters been left forsaken in the street?" It hardened her heart—it almost reconciled her to deceiving him—when he set his relatives up as patterns for her. Would he never understand that women detested having other women exhibited as examples to them? She looked round at him with a sense of impatient wonder. He was sitting at the luncheon-table, with his back turned on her, and his head resting on his hand. If he had attempted to rejoin her, she would have repelled him; if he had spoken, she would have met him with a sharp reply. He sat apart from her without uttering a word. In a man's hands silence is the most terrible of all protests, to the woman who loves him. Violence she can endure. Words she is always ready to meet by words on her side. Silence conquers her. After a moment's hesitation, Mercy left the sofa, and advanced submissively towards the table. She had offended him—and she alone was in fault. How should he know it, poor fellow, when he innocently mortified her? Step by step, she drew closer and closer. He never looked round; he never moved. She laid her hand timidly on his shoulder. "Forgive me, Horace," she whispered in his ear. "I am suffering this morning; I am not myself. I didn't mean what I said. Pray forgive me." There was no resisting the caressing tenderness of voice and manner which accompanied those words. He looked up; he took her hand. She bent over him, and touched his forehead with her lips. "Am I forgiven?" she asked.

"Oh, my darling," he said, "if you only knew how I loved you!"

"I do know it," she answered gently, twining his hair round her finger, and arranging it over his forehead where his hand had ruffled it.

They were completely absorbed in each other, or they must, at that moment, have heard the library door open at the other end of the room.

Lady Janet had written the necessary reply to her nephew, and had returned, faithful to her engagement, to plead the cause of Horace. The first object that met her view was her client pleading, with conspicuous success, for himself! "I am not wanted, evidently," thought the old lady. She noiselessly closed the door again, and left the lovers by themselves.

Horace returned, with unwise persistency, to the question of the deferred marriage. At the first words that he spoke, she drew back directly—sadly, not angrily.

"Don't press me to-day," she said; "I am not well to-day."

He rose, and looked at her anxiously. "May I speak about it to-morrow?"

"Yes, to-morrow." She returned to the sofa, and changed the subject. "What a time Lady Janet is away," she said. "What can be keeping her so long?"

Horace did his best to appear interested in the question of Lady Janet's prolonged absence. "What made her leave you?" he asked, standing at the back of the sofa and leaning over her.

"She went into the library to write a note to her nephew. By-the-by, who is her nephew?"

"Is it possible you don't know?"

"Indeed I don't."

"You have heard of him, no doubt," said Horace. "Lady Janet's nephew is a celebrated man." He paused, and stooping nearer to her, lifted a love-lock that lay over her shoulder, and pressed it to his lips. "Lady Janet's nephew," he resumed, "is Julian Gray."

She suddenly looked round at him in blank, bewildered terror, as if she doubted the evidence of her own senses.

Horace was completely taken by surprise. "My dear Grace!" he exclaimed; "what have I said or done to startle you this time?"

She held up her hand for silence. "Lady Janet's nephew is Julian Gray," she repeated slowly; "and I only know it now!"

Horace's perplexity increased. "My darling, now you do know it, what is there to alarm you?" he asked.

(There was enough to alarm the boldest woman living—in such a position, and with such a temperament as hers. To her mind, the personation of Grace Roseberry had assumed the aspect of a fatality. What lesser influence could have led her blindfold to the house in which she and the preacher at the Refuge were to meet? He was coming—the man who had reached her inmost heart, who had influenced her whole life! Was the day of reckoning coming with him?)

"Don't notice me," she said, faintly. "I have been ill all the morning. You saw it yourself when you came in here; even the sound of your voice alarmed

me. I shall be better directly. I am afraid I startled
you?"

"My dear Grace, it almost looked as if you were
terrified at the sound of Julian's name! He is a
public celebrity, I know; and I have seen ladies start
and stare at him when he entered a room. But *you*
looked perfectly panic-stricken."

She rallied her courage by a desperate effort; she
laughed—a harsh, uneasy laugh—and stopped him by
putting her hand over his mouth. "Absurd!" she said
lightly. "As if Mr. Julian Gray had anything to do
with my looks! I am better already. See for yourself!" She looked round at him again with a ghastly
gaiety; and returned, with a desperate assumption of
indifference, to the subject of Lady Janet's nephew.
"Of course I have heard of him," she said. "Do you
know that he is expected here to-day? Don't stand
there behind me—it's so hard to talk to you. Come
and sit down."   .

He obeyed—but she had not quite satisfied him
yet. His face had not lost its expression of anxiety
and surprise. She persisted in playing her part; determined to set at rest in him any possible suspicion
that she had reasons of her own for being afraid of

Julian Gray. "Tell me about this famous man of yours," she said, putting her arm familiarly through his arm. "What is he like?"

The caressing action and the easy tone had their effect on Horace. His face began to clear; he answered her lightly on his side.

"Prepare yourself to meet the most unclerical of clergymen," he said. "Julian is a lost sheep among the parsons, and a thorn in the side of his bishop. Preaches, if they ask him, in Dissenters' chapels. Declines to set up any pretensions to priestly authority and priestly power. Goes about doing good on a plan of his own. Is quite resigned never to rise to the high places in his profession. Says it's rising high enough for *him* to be the Archdeacon of the afflicted, the Dean of the hungry, and the Bishop of the poor. With all his oddities, as good a fellow as ever lived. Immensely popular with the women. They all go to him for advice. I wish you would go too."

Mercy changed colour. "What do you mean?" she asked sharply.

"Julian is famous for his powers of persuasion," said Horace, smiling. "If *he* spoke to you, Grace, he

8*

would prevail on you to fix the day. Suppose I ask
Julian to plead for me?"

He made the proposal in jest. Mercy's unquiet
mind accepted it as addressed to her in earnest. "He
will do it," she thought, with a sense of indescribable
terror, "if I don't stop him!" There was but one
chance for her. The only certain way to prevent
Horace from appealing to his friend, was to grant
what Horace wished for before his friend entered the
house.' She laid her hand on his shoulder; she
hid the terrible anxieties that were devouring her,
under an assumption of coquetry painful and pitiable
to see.

"Don't talk nonsense!" she said, gaily. "What
were we saying just now—before we began to speak
of Mr. Julian Gray?"

"We were wondering what had become of Lady
Janet," Horace replied.

She tapped him impatiently on the shoulder.
"No! no! It was something you said before that."

Her eyes completed what her words had left un-
spoken. Horace's arm stole round her waist.

"I was saying that I loved you," he answered, in
a whisper.

"Only that?"

"Are you tired of hearing it?"

She smiled charmingly. "Are you so very much in earnest about—about——?" She stopped, and looked away from him.

"About our marriage?"

"Yes."

"It is the one dearest wish of my life."

"Really?"

"Really!"

There was a pause. Mercy's fingers toyed nervously with the trinkets at her watch-chain. "When would you like it to be?" she said very softly, with her whole attention fixed on the watch-chain.

She had never spoken, she had never looked, as she spoke and looked now. Horace was afraid to believe in his own good fortune. "Oh, Grace!" he exclaimed, "you are not trifling with me?"

"What makes you think I am trifling with you?"

Horace was innocent enough to answer her seriously. "You would not even let me speak of our marriage just now," he said.

"Never mind what I did just now," she retorted,

petulantly. "They say women are changeable. It is one of the defects of the sex."

"Heaven be praised for the defects of the sex!" cried Horace, with devout sincerity. "Do you really leave me to decide?"

"If you insist on it."

Horace considered for a moment—the subject being the law of marriage. "We may be married by licence in a fortnight," he said. "I fix this day fortnight."

She held up her hands in protest.

"Why not? My lawyer is ready. There are no preparations to make. You said when you accepted me that it was to be a private marriage."

Mercy was obliged to own that she had certainly said that.

"We might be married at once—if the law would only let us. This day fortnight! Say—yes!" He drew her closer to him. There was a pause. The mask of coquetry—badly worn from the first—dropped from her. Her sad grey eyes rested compassionately on his eager face. "Don't look so serious!" he said. "Only one little word, Grace! Only Yes."

She sighed, and said it. He kissed her passion-

ately. It was only by a resolute effort that she released herself. "Leave me!" she said, faintly. "Pray
leave me by myself!"

She was in earnest—strangely in earnest. She was
trembling from head to foot. Horace rose to leave
her. "I will find Lady Janet," he said; "I long to
show the dear old lady that I have recovered my spirits,
and to tell her why." He turned round at the library
door. "You won't go away? You will let me see you
again when you are more composed?"

"I will wait here," said Mercy.

Satisfied with that reply, he left the room.

Her hands dropped on her lap; her head sank
back wearily on the cushions at the head of the sofa.
There was a dazed sensation in her: her mind felt
stunned. She wondered vacantly whether she was
awake or dreaming. Had she really said the word
which pledged her to marry Horace Holmcroft in a
fortnight? A fortnight! Something might happen in
that time to prevent it: she might find her way in a
fortnight out of the terrible position in which she stood.
Anyway, come what might of it, she had chosen the
preferable alternative to a private interview with Julian
Gray. She raised herself from her recumbent posi-

tion with a start, as the idea of the interview—dismissed for the last few minutes—possessed itself again of her mind. Her excited imagination figured Julian Gray as present in the room at that moment, speaking to her as Horace had proposed. She saw him seated close at her side—this man who had shaken her to the soul when he was in the pulpit, and when she was listening to him (unseen) at the other end of the chapel —she saw him close by her, looking her searchingly in the face; seeing her shameful secret in her eyes; hearing it in her voice; feeling it in her trembling hands; forcing it out of her word by word, till she fell prostrate at his feet with the confession of the fraud. Her head dropped again on the cushions; she hid her face in horror of the scene which her excited fancy had conjured up. Even now, when she had made that dreaded interview needless, could she feel sure (meeting him only on the most distant terms) of not betraying herself? She could *not* feel sure. Something in her shuddered and shrank at the bare idea of finding herself in the same room with him. She felt it, she knew it: her guilty conscience owned and feared its master in Julian Gray!

The minutes passed. The violence of her agitation began to tell physically on her weakened frame.

She found herself crying silently without knowing why. A weight was on her head, a weariness was in all her limbs. She sank lower on the cushions—her eyes closed—the monotonous ticking of the clock on the mantel-piece grew drowsily fainter and fainter on her ear. Little by little she dropped into slumber; slumber so light that she started when a morsel of coal fell into the grate, or when the birds chirped and twittered in their aviary in the winter-garden.

Lady Janet and Horace came in. She was faintly conscious of persons in the room. After an interval she opened her eyes, and half rose to speak to them. The room was empty again. They had stolen out softly, and left her to repose. Her eyes closed once more. She dropped back into slumber, and from slumber, in the favouring warmth and quiet of the place, into deep and dreamless sleep.

CHAPTER VIII.

The Man appears.

AFTER an interval of rest, Mercy was aroused by
the shutting of a glass door at the far end of the conservatory. This door, leading into the garden, was
used only by the inmates of the house, or by old
friends privileged to enter the reception-rooms by that
way. Assuming that either Horace or Lady Janet were
returning to the dining-room, Mercy raised herself a
little on the sofa and listened.

The voice of one of the men-servants caught her
ear. It was answered by another voice, which instantly set her trembling in every limb.

She started up, and listened again in breathless
terror. Yes! there was no mistaking it. The voice
that was answering the servant, was the unforgotten
voice which she had heard at the Refuge. The visitor
who had come in by the glass door was—Julian Gray!

His rapid footsteps advanced nearer and nearer to
the dining-room. She recovered herself sufficiently to

hurry to the library door. Her hand shook so that she failed at first to open it. She had just succeeded when she heard him again—speaking to her.

"Pray don't run away! I am nothing very formidable. Only Lady Janet's nephew—Julian Gray."

She turned slowly, spell-bound by his voice, and confronted him in silence.

He was standing, hat in hand, at the entrance to the conservatory, dressed in black, and wearing a white cravat—but with a studious avoidance of anything specially clerical in the make and form of his clothes. Young as he was, there were marks of care already on his face, and the hair was prematurely thin and scanty over his forehead. His slight active figure was of no more than the middle height. His complexion was pale. The lower part of his face, without beard or whiskers, was in no way remarkable. An average observer would have passed him by without notice—but for his eyes. These alone made a marked man of him. The unusual size of the orbits in which they were set, was enough of itself to attract attention; it gave a grandeur to his head, which the head, broad and firm as it was, did not possess. As to the eyes themselves, the soft lustrous brightness of them defied analysis. No two people could agree about their colour; divided opinion declaring alternately that they were dark grey or black. Painters had tried to reproduce them, and had given up the effort, in despair of seizing any one expression in the bewildering variety of expressions which they presented to view. They were eyes that could charm at one moment, and terrify at another; eyes that could set people laughing or crying almost at will. In action and in repose they were irresistible alike. When they first descried Mercy running to the door, they brightened gaily with the merriment of a child. When she turned and faced him, they changed instantly; softening and glowing as they mutely owned the interest and the admiration which the first sight of her had roused in him. His tone and manner altered at the same time. He addressed her with the deepest respect when he spoke his next words.

"Let me entreat you to favour me by resuming your seat," he said. "And let me ask your pardon if I have thoughtlessly intruded on you."

He paused, waiting for her reply before he advanced into the room. Still spell-bound by his voice, she recovered self-control enough to bow to him and to resume her place on the sofa. It was impossible to leave her now. After looking at her for a moment, he entered the room without speaking to her again. She was beginning to perplex as well as to interest him. "No common sorrow," he thought, "has set its mark on that woman's face; no common heart beats in that woman's breast. Who can she be?"

Mercy rallied her courage, and forced herself to speak to him.

"Lady Janet is in the library, I believe," she said timidly. "Shall I tell her you are here?"

"Don't disturb Lady Janet, and don't disturb yourself." With that answer he approached the luncheon-table, delicately giving her time to feel more at her ease. He took up what Horace had left of the bottle of claret, and poured it into a glass. "My aunt's claret shall represent my aunt for the present," he said, smiling, as he turned towards her once more. "I have had a long walk, and I may venture to help myself in this house without invitation. Is it useless to offer you anything?"

Mercy made the necessary reply. She was beginning already, after her remarkable experience of him, to wonder at his easy manners and his light way of talking.

He emptied his glass with the air of a man who thoroughly understood and enjoyed good wine. "My aunt's claret is worthy of my aunt," he said, with comic gravity, as he set down the glass. "Both are the genuine products of Nature." He seated himself at the table, and looked critically at the different dishes left on it. One dish especially attracted his attention. "What is this?" he went on. "A French pie! It seems grossly unfair to taste French wine, and to pass over French pie without notice." He took up a knife and fork, and enjoyed the pie as critically as he had enjoyed the wine. "Worthy of the Great Nation!" he exclaimed with enthusiasm. "*Vive la France!*"

Mercy listened and looked, in inexpressible astonishment. He was utterly unlike the picture which her fancy had drawn of him in everyday life. Take off his white cravat, and nobody would have discovered that this famous preacher was a clergyman!

He helped himself to another plateful of the pie, and spoke more directly to Mercy; alternately eating and talking as composedly and pleasantly as if they had known each other for years.

. "I came here by way of Kensington Gardens," he said. "For some time past I have been living in a flat, ugly, barren agricultural district. You can't think how pleasant I found the picture presented by the Gardens, as a contrast. The ladies in their rich winter dresses, the smart nursery maids, the lovely children, the ever-moving crowd skating on the ice of the Round Pond; it was all so 'exhilarating after what I have been used io, that I actually caught myself whistling as I walked through the brilliant scene! (In my time boys used always to whistle when they were in good spirits, and I have not got over the habit yet.) Who do you think I met when I was in full song?"

As well as her amazement would let her, Mercy excused herself from guessing. She had never in all her life before spoken to any living being so confusedly and so unintelligently as she now spoke to Julian Gray!

He went on more gaily than ever, without appearing to notice the effect that he had produced on her.

"Whom did I meet," he repeated, "when I was in full song? My bishop! If I had been whistling a sacred melody, his lordship might perhaps have excused my vulgarity out of consideration for my music. Unfortunately, the composition I was executing at the moment (I am one of the loudest of living whistlers) was by Verdi—'*La Donna e Mobile*'—familiar, no doubt, to his lordship on the street organs. He recognised the tune, poor man, and when I took off my hat to him he looked the other way. Strange, in a world that is bursting with sin and sorrow, to treat such a trifle seriously as a cheerful clergyman whistling a tune!" He pushed away his plate as he said the last words, and went on simply and earnestly in an altered tone. "I have never been able," he said, "to see why we should assert ourselves among other men as belonging to a particular caste, and as being forbidden, in any harmless thing, to do as other people do. The disciples of old set us no such example; they were wiser and better than we are. I venture to say, that one of the worst obstacles in the way of our doing good among our fellow creatures is raised by the mere assumption of the clerical manner and the clerical voice. For my part, I set up no claim to be more sacred and more reverend than any other Christian man who does what good he can." He glanced brightly at Mercy, looking at him in helpless perplexity. The spirit of fun took possession of him again. "Are you a Radical?" he asked, with a humorous twinkle in his large lustrous eyes. "I am!"

Mercy tried hard to understand him, and tried in vain. Could this be the preacher whose words had charmed, purified, ennobled her? Was this the man whose sermon had drawn tears from women about her whom she knew to be shameless and hardened in crime? Yes! The eyes that now rested on her humorously, were the beautiful eyes which had looked into her soul. The voice that had just addressed a jesting question to her, was the deep and mellow voice which had once thrilled her to the heart. In the pulpit, he was an angel of mercy; out of the pulpit, he was a boy let loose from school.

"Don't let me startle you!" he said, good-naturedly noticing her confusion. "Public opinion has called me by harder names than the name of 'Radical.' I have been spending my time lately—as I told you just now—in an agricultural district. My business there was to perform the duty for the rector of the place, who wanted a holiday. How do you think the ex-, periment has ended? The Squire of the parish calls me a Communist; the farmers denounce me as an Incendiary; my friend the rector has been recalled in a hurry; and I have now the honour of speaking to you in the character of a banished man, who has made a respectable neighbourhood too hot to hold him."

With that frank avowal, he left the luncheon-table, and took a chair near Mercy.

"You will naturally be anxious," he went on, "to know what my offence was. Do you understand Political Economy and the Laws of Supply and Demand?"

Mercy owned that she did *not* understand them.

"No more do I—in a Christian country," he said. "That was my offence. You shall hear my confession (just as my aunt will hear it) in two words." He paused for a little while; his variable manner changed again. Mercy, shyly looking at him, saw a new expression in his eyes—an expression which recalled her first remembrance of him as nothing had recalled it yet. "I had no idea," he resumed, "of what the life of a farm-labourer really was, in some parts of England, until I undertook the rector's duties. Never before had I seen such dire wretchedness as I saw in the cottages. Never before had I met with such noble patience under suffering as I found among the people. The martyrs of old could endure, and die. I asked myself if they could endure, and *live*, like the martyrs whom I saw round me?—live, week after week, month after month, year after year, on the brink of starvation; live, and see their pining children growing up round them, to work and want in their turn; live, with the poor man's parish-prison to look to as the end, when hunger and labour have done their worst! Was God's beautiful earth made to hold such misery as this? I can hardly think of it, I can hardly speak of it, even now, with dry eyes!"

His head sank on his breast. He waited—mastering his emotion before he spoke again. Now, at last, she knew him once more. Now he was the man, indeed, whom she had expected to see. Unconsciously, she sat listening, with her eyes fixed on his face, with her heart hanging on his words, in the very attitude of the bygone day, when she had heard him for the first time! ·

"I did all I could to plead for the helpless ones,"

9*

he resumed. "I went round among the holders of the land to say a word for the tillers of the land. 'These patient people don't want much' (I said); 'in the name of Christ, give them enough to live on!' Political Economy shrieked at the horrid proposal; the Laws of Supply and Demand veiled their majestic faces in dismay. Starvation wages were the right wages, I was told. And why? Because the labourer was obliged to accept them! I determined, so far as one man could do it, that the labourer should *not* be obliged to accept them. I collected my own resources—I wrote to my friends—and I removed some of the poor fellows to parts of England where their work was better paid. Such was the conduct which made the neighbourhood too hot to hold me. So let it be! I mean to go on. I am known in London; I can raise subscriptions. The vile Laws of Supply and Demand shall find labour scarce in that agricultural district; and pitiless Political Economy shall spend a few extra shillings on the poor, as certainly as I am that Radical, Communist, and Incendiary—Julian Gray!"

He rose—making a little gesture of apology for the warmth with which he had spoken—and took a turn in the room. Fired by *his* enthusiasm, Mercy followed him. Her purse was in her hand, when he turned and faced her.

"Pray let me offer my little tribute—such as it is!" she said, eagerly.

A momentary flush spread over his pale cheeks as he looked at the beautiful compassionate face pleading with him.

"No! no!" he said, smiling, "though I *am* a parson, I don't carry the begging-box everywhere." Mercy attempted to press the purse on him. The quaint humour began to twinkle again in his eyes as he abruptly drew back from it. "Don't tempt me!" he said. "The frailest of all human creatures is a clergyman tempted by a subscription." Mercy persisted, and conquered; she made him prove the truth of his own profound observation of clerical human nature by taking a piece of money from the purse. "If I must take it—I must!" he remarked. "Thank you for setting the good example! thank you for giving the timely help! What name shall I put down on my list?"

Mercy's eyes looked confusedly away from him. "No name," she said, in a low voice. "My subscription is anonymous."

As she replied, the library door opened. To her

infinite relief—to Julian's secret disappointment—Lady
Janet Roy and Horace Holmcroft entered the room
together.

"Julian!" exclaimed Lady Janet, holding up her
hands in astonishment.

He kissed his aunt on the cheek. "Your ladyship
is looking charmingly." He gave his hand to Horace.
Horace took it, and passed on to Mercy. They walked
away together slowly to the other end of the room.
Julian seized on the chance which left him free to
speak privately to his aunt.

"I came in through the conservatory," he said. "And
I found that young lady in the room. Who is she?"

"Are you very much interested in her?" asked
Lady Janet, in her gravely ironical way.

Julian answered in one expressive word. "Indescribably!"

Lady Janet called to Mercy to join her.

"My dear," she said, "let me formally present my
nephew to you. Julian, this is Miss Grace Roseberry——" She suddenly checked herself. The instant she pronounced the name, Julian started as if it
was a surprise to him. "What is it?" she asked, sharply.

"Nothing," he answered, bowing to Mercy, with a

marked absence of his former ease of manner. She
returned the courtesy a little restrainedly on her side.
She too had seen him start when Lady Janet mentioned the name by which she was known. The start
meant something. What could it be? Why did he
turn aside, after bowing to her, and address himself
to Horace, with an absent look in his face, as if his
thoughts were far away from his words? A complete
change had come over him; and it dated from the
moment when his aunt had pronounced the name
that was not *her* name—the name that she had stolen!

Lady Janet claimed Julian's attention, and left
Horace free to return to Mercy. "Your room is ready
for you," she said. "You will stay here, of course?"
Julian accepted the invitation—still with the air of a
man whose mind was pre-occupied. Instead of looking at his aunt when he made his reply, he looked
round at Mercy, with a troubled curiosity in his face,
very strange to see. Lady Janet tapped him impatiently on the shoulder. "I expect people to look
at me when people speak to me," she said. "What
are you staring at my adopted daughter for?"

"Your adopted daughter?" Julian repeated—looking at his aunt this time, and looking very earnestly.

"Certainly! As Colonel Roseberry's daughter, she is connected with me by marriage already. Did you think I had picked up a foundling?"

Julian's face cleared; he looked relieved. "I had forgotten the Colonel," he answered. "Of course the young lady is related to us, as you say."

"Charmed, I am sure, to have satisfied you that Grace is not an impostor," said Lady Janet, with satirical humility. She took Julian's arm, and drew him out of hearing of Horace and Mercy. "About that letter of yours?" she proceeded. "There is one line in it that rouses my curiosity. Who is the mysterious 'lady' whom you wish to present to me?"

Julian started, and changed colour.

"I can't tell you now," he said, in a whisper.

"Why not?"

To Lady Janet's unutterable astonishment, instead of replying, Julian looked round at her adopted daughter once more.

"What has *she* got to do with it?" asked the old lady, out of all patience with him.

"It is impossible for me to tell you," he answered gravely, "while Miss Roseberry is in the room."

CHAPTER IX.

News from Mannheim.

LADY JANET'S curiosity was by this time thoroughly aroused. Summoned to explain who the nameless lady mentioned in his letter could possibly be, Julian had looked at her adopted daughter. Asked next to explain what her adopted daughter had to do with it, he had declared that he could not answer while Miss Roseberry was in the room.

What did he mean? Lady Janet determined to find out.

"I hate all mysteries," she said to Julian. "And as for secrets, I consider them to be one of the forms of ill-breeding. People in our rank of life ought to be above whispering in corners. If you *must* have your mystery, I can offer you a corner in the library. Come with me."

Julian followed his aunt very reluctantly. Whatever the mystery might be, he was plainly embarrassed by being called upon to reveal it at a moment's notice. Lady Janet settled herself in her chair, pre-

pared to question and cross-question her nephew—
when an obstacle appeared at the other end of the
library, in the shape of a man-servant with a message. One of Lady Janet's neighbours had called
by appointment to take her to the meeting of a certain committee which assembled that day. The servant announced that the neighbour—an elderly lady
—was then waiting in her carriage at the door.

Lady Janet's ready invention set the obstacle
aside without a moment's delay. She directed the
servant to show her visitor into the drawing-room,
and to say that she was unexpectedly engaged, but
that Miss Roseberry would see the lady immediately.
She then turned to Julian, and said, with her most
satirical emphasis of tone and manner, "Would it be
an additional convenience if Miss Roseberry was not
only out of the room before you disclose your secret,
but out of the house?"

Julian gravely answered, "It may possibly be quite
as well if Miss Roseberry is out of the house."

Lady Janet led the way back to the dining-room.

"My dear Grace," she said, "you looked flushed
and feverish when I saw you asleep on the sofa a
little while since. It will do you no harm to have a

drive in the fresh air. Our friend has called to take
me to the committee meeting. I have sent to tell her
that I am engaged—and I shall be much obliged if
you will go in my place."

Mercy looked a little alarmed. "Does your ladyship mean the committee meeting of the Samaritan
Convalescent Home? The members, as I understand
it, are to decide to-day which of the plans for the
new building they are to adopt. I cannot surely pre-
sume to vote in your place?"

"You can vote, my dear child, just as well as I
can," replied the old lady. "Architecture is one of
the lost arts. You know nothing about it; I know
nothing about it; the architects themselves know nothing about it. One plan is no doubt just as bad as
the other. Vote, as I should vote, with the majority.
Or as poor dear Dr. Johnson said, 'Shout with the
loudest mob.' Away with you—and don't keep the
committee waiting."

Horace hastened to open the door for Mercy.

"How long shall you be away?" he whispered
confidentially. "I had a thousand things to say to
you, and they have interrupted us."

"I shall be back in an hour."

"We shall have the room to ourselves by that time. Come here when you return. You will find me waiting for you."

Mercy pressed his hand significantly, and went out. Lady Janet turned to Julian, who had thus far remained in the background, still, to all appearance, as unwilling as ever to enlighten his aunt.

"Well?" she said. "What is tying your tongue now? Grace is out of the room; why don't you begin? Is Horace in the way?"

"Not in the least. I am only a little uneasy——"

"Uneasy about what?"

"I am afraid you have put that charming creature to some inconvenience in sending her away just at this time."

Horace looked up suddenly with a flush on his face.

"When you say 'that charming creature,'" he asked sharply, "I suppose you mean Miss Roseberry?"

"Certainly," answered Julian. "Why not?"

Lady Janet interposed. "Gently, Julian," she said. "Grace has only been introduced to you hitherto in the character of my adopted daughter——"

"And it seems to be high time," Horace added

haughtily, "that I should present her next in the character of my engaged wife."

Julian looked at Horace as if he could hardly credit the evidence of his own ears. "Your wife!" he exclaimed with an irrepressible outburst of disappointment and surprise.

"Yes. My wife," returned Horace. "We are to be married in a fortnight. May I ask," he added, with angry humility, "if you disapprove of the marriage?"

Lady Janet interposed once more. "Nonsense, Horace," she said. "Julian congratulates you, of course."

Julian coldly and absently echoed the words. "Oh, yes! I congratulate you, of course."

Lady Janet returned to the main object of the interview.

"Now we thoroughly understand one another," she said, "let us speak of a lady who has dropped out of the conversation for the last minute or two. I mean, Julian, the mysterious lady of your letter. We are alone, as you desired. Lift the veil, my reverend nephew, which hides her from mortal eyes! Blush, if you like—and can. Is she the future Mrs. Julian Gray?"

"She is a perfect stranger to me," Julian answered, quietly.

"A perfect stranger!   You wrote me word you were interested in her."

"I *am* interested in her.   And, what is more, you are interested in her, too."

Lady Janet's fingers drummed impatiently on the table.   "Have I not warned you, Julian, that I hate mysteries?   Will you, or will you not, explain yourself?"

Before it was possible to answer, Horace rose from his chair.   "Perhaps I am in the way?" he said.

Julian signed to him to sit down again.

"I have already told Lady Janet that you are not in the way," he answered.   "I now tell *you*—as Miss Roseberry's future husband—that you too have an interest in hearing what I have to say."

Horace resumed his seat with an air of suspicious surprise.   Julian addressed himself to Lady Janet.

"You have often heard me speak," he began, "of an old friend of mine, who had an appointment abroad?"

"Yes.   The English consul at Mannheim?"

"The same. When I returned from the country, I found among my other letters, a long letter from the consul. I have brought it with me, and I propose to read certain passages from it, which tell a very strange story more plainly and more credibly than I can tell it in my own words."

"Will it be very long?" inquired Lady Janet, looking with some alarm at the closely written sheets of paper which her nephew spread open before him.

Horace followed with a question on his side.

"You are sure I am interested in it?" he asked. "The consul at Mannheim is a total stranger to me."

"I answer for it," replied Julian, gravely, "neither my aunt's patience nor yours, Horace, will be thrown away if you will favour me by listening attentively to what I am about to read."

With those words he began his first extract from the consul's letter.

* * * "'My memory is a bad one for dates. But full three months must have passed since information was sent to me of an English patient, received at the hospital here, whose case I, as English consul, might feel an interest in investigating.

"'I went the same day to the hospital, and was taken to the bed-side.

"'The patient was a woman—young, and (when in health) I should think, very pretty. When I first saw her she looked, to my uninstructed eye, like a dead woman. I noticed that her head had a bandage over it, and I asked what was the nature of the injury that she had received. The answer informed me that the poor creature had been present, nobody knew why or wherefore, at a skirmish or night attack between the Germans and the French, and that the injury to her head had been inflicted by a fragment of a German shell.'"

Horace—thus far leaning back carelessly in his chair—suddenly raised himself and exclaimed, "Good heavens! can this be the woman I saw laid out for dead in the French cottage?"

"It is impossible for me to say," replied Julian. "Listen to the rest of it. The consul's letter may answer your question."

He went on with his reading:

"'The wounded woman had been reported dead, and had been left by the French in their retreat, at the time when the German forces took possession of the enemy's position. She was found on a bed in a cottage by the director of the German ambulance——"

"Ignatius Wetzel!" cried Horace.

"Ignatius Wetzel," repeated Julian, looking at the letter.

"It *is* the same!" said Horace. "Lady Janet, we are really interested in this. You remember my telling you how I first met with Grace? And you have heard more about it since, no doubt, from Grace herself?"

"She has a horror of referring to that part of her journey home," replied Lady Janet. "She mentioned her having been stopped on the frontier, and her finding herself accidentally in the company of another Englishwoman, a perfect stranger to her. I naturally asked questions on my side, and was shocked to hear that she had seen the woman killed by a German shell almost close at her side. Neither she nor I have had any relish for returning to the subject since. You were quite right, Julian, to avoid speaking of it while she was in the room. I understand it all now. Grace, I suppose, mentioned my name and her name to her fellow-traveller. The woman is in want of assistance, and she applies to me through you. I will help her; but she must not come here until I have prepared

Grace 'for seeing her again, a living woman. For the present, there is no reason why they should meet."

"I am not sure about that," said Julian, in low tones, without looking up at his aunt.

"What do you mean? Is the mystery not at an end yet?"

"The mystery is not even begun yet. Let my friend the consul proceed."

Julian returned for the second time to his extract from the letter.

"'After a careful examination of the supposed corpse, the German surgeon arrived at the conclusion that a case of suspended animation had (in the hurry of the French retreat) been mistaken for a case of death. Feeling a professional interest in the subject, he decided on putting his opinion to the test. He operated on the patient with complete success. After performing the operation, he kept her for some days under his own care, and then transferred her to the nearest hospital—the hospital at Mannheim. He was obliged to return to his duties as army surgeon, and he left his patient in the condition in which I saw her, insensible on the bed. Neither he nor the hospital authorities knew anything whatever about the woman.

No papers were found on her. All the doctors could do, when I asked them for information with a view to communicating with her friends, was to show me her linen marked with her name. I left the hospital after taking down the name in my pocket-book. It was 'Mercy Merrick.'"

Lady Janet produced *her* pocket-book. "Let me take the name down too," she said. "I never heard it before, and I might otherwise forget it. Go on, Julian."

Julian advanced to his second extract from the consul's letter:

"'Under these circumstances, I could only wait to hear from the hospital when the patient was sufficiently recovered to be able to speak to me. Some weeks passed without my receiving any communication from the doctors. On calling to make enquiries, I was informed that fever had set in, and that the poor creature's condition now alternated between exhaustion and delirium. In her delirious moments, the name of your aunt, Lady Janet Roy, frequently escaped her. Otherwise, her wanderings were for the most part quite unintelligible to the people at her bedside. I thought once or twice of writing to you

10*

and of begging you to speak to Lady Janet. But as
the doctors informed me that the chances of life or
death were at this time almost equally balanced, I
decided to wait until time should determine whether
it was necessary to trouble you or not.'"

"You know best, Julian," said Lady Janet. "But
I own I don't quite see in what way I am interested in
this part of the story."

"Just what I was going to say," added Horace.
"It is very sad, no doubt. But what have *we* to do
with it?"

"Let me read my third extract," Julian answered,
"and you will see."

He turned to the third extract, and read as follows:

"'At last I received a message from the hospital
informing me that Mercy Merrick was out of danger,
and that she was capable (though still very weak) of
answering any questions which I might think it desirable to put to her. On reaching the hospital, I was
requested, rather to my surprise, to pay my first visit
to the head physician in his private room. "I think
it right," said this gentleman, "to warn you, before
you see the patient, to be very careful how you speak

to her, and not to irritate her by showing any surprise
or expressing any doubts if she talks to you in an
extravagant manner. We differ in opinion about her
here. Some of us (myself among the number) doubt
whether the recovery of her mind has accompanied
the recovery of her bodily powers. Without pro-
nouncing her to be mad—she is perfectly gentle and
harmless—we are nevertheless of opinion that she is
suffering under a species of insane delusion. Bear in
mind the caution which I have given you—and now
go and judge for yourself." I obeyed, in some little
perplexity and surprise. The sufferer, when I approached her bed, looked sadly weak and worn; but,
so far as I could judge, seemed to be in full possession of herself. Her tone and manner were unques-
tionably the tone and manner of a lady. After briefly
introducing myself, I assured her that I should be
glad, both officially and personally, if I could be of
any assistance to her. In saying these trifling words,
I happened to address her by the name I had seen
marked on her clothes. The instant the words "Miss
Merrick" passed my lips, a wild, vindictive expression
appeared in her eyes. She exclaimed angrily, "Don't
call me by that hateful name! It's not my name. All

the people here persecute me by calling me Mercy
Merrick. And when I am angry with them they show
me the clothes. Say what I may, they persist in believing they are *my* clothes. Don't you do the same,
if you want to be friends with me." Remembering
what the physician had said, I made the necessary
excuses, and soon succeeded in soothing her. Without
reverting to the irritating topic of the name, I merely
enquired what her plans were, and assured her that
she might command my services if she required them.
"Why do you want to know what my plans are?" she
asked suspiciously. I reminded her in reply that I
held the position of English consul, and that my object was, if possible, to be of some assistance to her.
"You can be of the greatest assistance to me," she
said eagerly. "Find Mercy Merrick!" I saw the vindictive look come back into her eyes, and an angry
flush rising on her white cheeks. Abstaining from
showing any surprise, I asked her who Mercy Merrick
was? "A vile woman, by her own confession," was
the quick reply. "How am I to find her?" I enquired
next. "Look for a woman in a black dress, with the
Red Geneva Cross on her shoulder; she is a nurse in
the French ambulance." "What has she done?" "I

have lost my papers; I have lost my own clothes; Mercy Merrick has taken them." "How do you know that Mercy Merrick has taken them?" "Nobody else could have taken them—that's how I know it. Do you believe me or not?" She was beginning to excite herself again; I assured her that I would at once send to make enquiries after Mercy Merrick. She turned round, contented, on the pillow. "There's a good man!" she said. "Come back and tell me when you have caught her." Such was my first interview with the English patient at the hospital at Mannheim. It is needless to say that I doubted the existence of the absent person described as a nurse. However, it was possible to make enquiries, by applying to the surgeon, Ignatius Wetzel, whose whereabouts was known to his friends in Mannheim. I wrote to him, and received his answer in due time. After the night attack of the Germans had made them masters of the French position, he had entered the cottage occupied by the French ambulance. He had found the wounded Frenchmen left behind, but had seen no such person in attendance on them as the nurse in the black dress, with the red cross on her shoulder. The only living woman in the place was a young English lady, in a

grey travelling cloak, who had been stopped on the
frontier, and who was forwarded on her way home by
the war-correspondent of an English journal.'"

"That was Grace," said Lady Janet.

"And I was the war-correspondent," added
Horace.

"A few words more," said Julian, "and you will
understand my object in claiming your attention."

He returned to the letter for the last time, and
concluded his extracts from it as follows:

"'Instead of attending at the hospital myself, I
communicated by letter the failure of my attempt to
discover the missing nurse. For some little time afterwards I heard no more of the sick woman, whom I
shall still call Mercy Merrick. It was only yesterday
that I received another summons to visit the patient.
She had by this time sufficiently recovered to claim
her discharge, and she had announced her intention
of returning forthwith to England. The head physician,
feeling a sense of responsibility, had sent for me. It
was impossible to detain her on the ground that she
was not fit to be trusted by herself at large, in
consequence of the difference of opinion among the
doctors on the case. All that could be done was to

give me due notice, and to leave the matter in my hands. On seeing her for the second time, I found her sullen and reserved. She openly attributed my inability to find the nurse to want of zeal for her interests on my part. I had, on my side, no authority whatever to detain her. I could only inquire whether she had money enough to pay her travelling expenses. Her reply informed me that the chaplain of the hospital had mentioned her forlorn situation in the town, and that the English residents had subscribed a small sum of money to enable her to return to her own country. Satisfied on this head, I asked next if she had friends to go to in England. "I have one friend," she answered, "who is a host in herself—Lady Janet Roy." You may imagine my surprise when I heard this. I found it quite useless to make any further inquiries as to how she came to know your aunt, whether your aunt expected her, and so on. My questions evidently offended her; they were received in sulky silence. Under these circumstances, well knowing that I can trust implicitly to your humane sympathy for misfortune, I have decided (after careful reflection) to ensure the poor creature's safety when she arrives in London, by giving her a letter to you.

You will hear what she says; and you will be better able to discover than I am whether she really has any claim on Lady Janet Roy. One last word of information, which it may be necessary to add—and I shall close this inordinately long letter. At my first interview with her I abstained, as I have already told you, from irritating her by any inquiries on the subject of her name. On this second occasion, however, I decided on putting the question.'"

As he read those last words, Julian became aware of a sudden movement on the part of his aunt. Lady Janet had risen softly from her chair, and had passed behind him with the purpose of reading the consul's letter for herself over her nephew's shoulder. Julian detected the action just in time to frustrate Lady Janet's intention, by placing his hand over the last two lines of the letter.

"What do you do that for?" inquired his aunt sharply.

"You are welcome, Lady Janet, to read the close of the letter for yourself," Julian replied. "But before you do so I am anxious to prepare you for a very great surprise. Compose yourself, and let me read on slowly, with your eye on me, until I uncover the last two words which close my friend's letter."

He read the end of the letter, as he had proposed, in these terms:

"'I looked the woman straight in the face, and I said to her, "You have denied that the name marked on the clothes which you wore when you came here was your name. If you are not Mercy Merrick, who are you?" She answered instantly, "My name is"'"——

Julian removed his hand from the page. Lady Janet looked at the next two words, and started back with a loud cry of astonishment which brought Horace instantly to his feet.

"Tell me, one of you!" he cried. "What name did she give?"

Julian told him:

"GRACE ROSEBERRY."

CHAPTER X.

A Council of Three.

FOR a moment Horace stood thunderstruck, looking in blank astonishment at Lady Janet. His first
words, as soon as he had recovered himself, were addressed to Julian:

"Is this a joke?" he asked, sternly. "If it is, I for
one don't see the humour of it."

Julian pointed to the closely written pages of the
consul's letter. "A man writes in earnest," he said,
"when he writes at such length as this. The woman
seriously gave the name of Grace Roseberry, and
when she left Mannheim she travelled to England for
the express purpose of presenting herself to Lady
Janet Roy." He turned to his aunt. "You saw me
start," he went on, "when you first mentioned Miss
Roseberry's name in my hearing. Now you know
why." He addressed himself once more to Horace.
"You heard me say that you, as Miss Roseberry's
future husband, had an interest in being present at
my interview with Lady Janet. Now *you* know why."

"The woman is plainly mad," said Lady Janet. "But it is certainly a startling form of madness when one first hears of it. Of course we must keep the matter, for the present at least, a secret from Grace."

"There can be no doubt," Horace agreed, "that Grace must be kept in the dark, in her present state of health. The servants had better be warned beforehand, in case of this adventuress or madwoman, whichever she may be, attempting to make her way into the house."

"It shall be done immediately," said Lady Janet. "What surprises *me*, Julian (ring the bell, if you please), is, that you should describe yourself in your letter as feeling an interest in this person."

Julian answered—without ringing the bell.

"I am more interested than ever," he said, "now I find that Miss Roseberry herself is your guest at Mablethorpe House."

"You were always perverse, Julian, as a child, in your likings and dislikings," Lady Janet rejoined. "Why don't you ring the bell?"

"For one good reason, my dear aunt. I don't wish to hear you tell your servants to close the door on this friendless creature."

Lady Janet cast a look at her nephew which
plainly expressed that she thought he had taken a
liberty with her.

"You don't expect me to see the woman?" she
asked, in a tone of cold surprise.

"I hope you will not refuse to see her," Julian answered quietly. " I was out when she called. I must
hear what she has to say—and I should infinitely
prefer hearing it in your presence. When I got your
reply to my letter, permitting me to present her to
you, I wrote to her immediately, appointing a meeting
here."

Lady Janet lifted her bright black eyes in mute
expostulation to the carved cupids and wreaths on the
dining-room ceiling.

"When am I to have the honour of the lady's
visit?" she inquired, with ironical resignation.

"'To-day," answered her nephew, with impenetrable
patience.

"At what hour?"

Julian composedly consulted his watch. "She is
ten minutes after her time," he said, and put his watch
back in his pocket again.

At the same moment the servant appeared, and

advanced to Julian, carrying a visiting card on his little silver tray.

"A lady to see you, sir."

Julian took the card, and, bowing, handed it to his aunt.

"Here she is," he said, just as quietly as ever.

Lady Janet looked at the card, and tossed it indignantly back to her nephew. "Miss Roseberry!" she exclaimed. "Printed, actually printed on her card! Julian, even MY patience has its limits. I refuse to see her!"

The servant was still waiting—not like a human being who took an interest in the proceedings—but (as became a perfectly bred footman) like an article of furniture artfully constructed to come and go at the word of command. Julian gave the word of command, addressing the admirably constructed automaton by the name of "James."

"Where is the lady, now?" he asked.

"In the breakfast-room, sir."

"Leave her there, if you please; and wait outside within hearing of the bell."

The legs of the furniture-footman acted, and took

him noiselessly out of the room. Julian turned to his aunt.

"Forgive me," he said, "for venturing to give the man his orders in your presence. I am very anxious that you should not decide hastily. Surely we ought to hear what this lady has to say?"

Horace dissented widely from his friend's opinion. "It's an insult to Grace," he broke out warmly, "to hear what she has to say!"

Lady Janet nodded her head in high approval. "I think so, too," said her ladyship, crossing her handsome old hands resolutely on her lap.

Julian applied himself to answering Horace first.

"Pardon me," he said, "I have no intention of presuming to reflect on Miss Roseberry, or of bringing her into the matter at all. The consul's letter," he went on, speaking to his aunt, "mentions, if you remember, that the medical authorities of Mannheim were divided in opinion on their patient's case. Some of them—the physician-in-chief being among the number—believe that the recovery of her mind has not accompanied the recovery of her body."

"In other words," Lady Janet remarked, "a madwoman is in my house, and I am expected to receive her!"

"Don't let us exaggerate," said Julian, gently. "It can serve no good interest, in this serious matter, to exaggerate anything. The consul assures us, on the authority of the doctor, that she is perfectly gentle and harmless. If she is really the victim of a mental delusion, the poor creature is surely an object of compassion, and she ought to be placed under proper care. Ask your own kind heart, my dear aunt, if it would not be downright cruelty to turn this forlorn woman adrift in the world, without making some inquiry first?"

Lady Janet's inbred sense of justice admitted—not over-willingly—the reasonableness as well as the humanity of the view expressed in those words. "There is some truth in that, Julian," she said, shifting her position uneasily in her chair, and looking at Horace. "Don't you think so too?" she added.

"I can't say I do," answered Horace, in the positive tone of a man whose obstinacy is proof against every form of appeal that can be addressed to him.

The patience of Julian was firm enough to be a match for the obstinacy of Horace. "At any rate," he resumed, with undiminished good temper, "we are all three equally interested in setting this matter at rest.

I put it to you, Lady Janet, if we are not favoured, at this lucky moment, with the very opportunity that we want? Miss Roseberry is not only out of the room, but out of the house. If we let this chance slip, who can say what awkward accident may not happen in the course of the next few days?"

"Let the woman come in," cried Lady Janet, deciding headlong with her customary impatience of all delay. "At once, Julian—before Grace can come back. Will you ring the bell this time?"

This time Julian rang it. "May I give the man his orders?" he respectfully inquired of his aunt.

"Give him anything you like, and have done with it!" retorted the irritable old lady, getting briskly on her feet, and taking a turn in the room to compose herself.

The servant withdrew, with orders to show the visitor in.

Horace crossed the room at the same time—apparently with the intention of leaving it by the door at the opposite end.

"You are not going away?" exclaimed Lady Janet.

"I see no use in my remaining here," replied Horace, not very graciously.

"In that case," retorted Lady Janet, "remain here because I wish it."

"Certainly —if you wish it. Only remember," he added, more obstinately than ever, "that I differ entirely from Julian's view. In my opinion the woman has no claim on us."

A passing movement of irritation escaped Julian for the first time. "Don't be hard, Horace," he said, sharply. "All women have a claim on us."

They had unconsciously gathered together, in the heat of the little debate, turning their backs on the library door. At the last words of the reproof administered by Julian to Horace, their attention was recalled to passing events by the slight noise produced by the opening and closing of the door. With one accord, the three turned and looked in the direction from which the sound had come.

CHAPTER XI.

The Dead alive.

JUST inside the door there appeared the figure of
a small woman dressed in plain and poor black garments. She silently lifted her black net veil, and disclosed a dull, pale, worn, weary face. The forehead
was low and broad; the eyes were unusually far apart;
the lower features were remarkably small and delicate.
In health (as the consul at Mannheim had remarked)
this woman must have possessed, if not absolute
beauty, at least rare attractions peculiarly her own.
As it was now, suffering—sullen, silent, self-contained
suffering—had marred its beauty. Attention and even
curiosity it might still rouse. Admiration or interest
it could excite no longer.

The small thin black figure stood immovably inside the door. The dull, worn, white face looked
silently at the three persons in the room.

The three persons in the room, on their side, stood
for a moment without moving, and looked silently at
the stranger on the threshold. There was something,

either in the woman herself or in the sudden and
stealthy manner of her appearance on the scene which
froze, as if with the touch of an invisible cold hand,
the sympathies of all three. Accustomed to the world,
habitually at their ease in every social emergency, they
were now silenced for the first time in their lives by
the first serious sense of embarrassment which they
had felt since they were children, in the presence of a
stranger.

Had the appearance of the true Grace Roseberry
aroused in their minds a suspicion of the woman who
had stolen her name, and taken her place in the
house?

Not so much as the shadow of a suspicion of
Mercy was at the bottom of the strange sense of un-
easiness which had now deprived them alike of their
habitual courtesy and their habitual presence of mind.
It was as practically impossible for any one of the
three to doubt the identity of the adopted daughter
of the house, as it would be for you who read these
lines to doubt the identity of the nearest and dearest
relative you have in the world. Circumstances had
fortified Mercy behind the strongest of all natural
rights—the right of first possession. Circumstances

had armed her with the most irresistible of all natural forces—the force of previous association and previous habit. Not by so much as a hair's breadth was the position of the false Grace Roseberry shaken by the first appearance of the true Grace Roseberry within the doors of Mablethorpe House. Lady Janet felt suddenly repelled, without knowing why. Julian and Horace felt suddenly repelled, without knowing why. Asked to describe their own sensations at the moment, they would have shaken their heads in despair, and would have answered in those words. The vague presentiment of some misfortune to come, had entered the room with the entrance of the woman in black. But it moved invisibly; and it spoke, as all presentiments speak, in the Unknown Tongue.

A moment passed. The crackling of the fire and the ticking of the clock were the only sounds audible in the room.

The voice of the visitor—hard, clear, and quiet—was the first voice that broke the silence.

"Mr. Julian Gray?" she said, looking interrogatively from one of the two gentlemen to the other.

Julian advanced a few steps, instantly recovering

his self-possession. "I am sorry I was not at home,"
he said, "when you called with your letter from the
consul. Pray take a chair."

By way of setting the example, Lady Janet seated
herself at some little distance, with Horace in attendance standing near. She bowed to the stranger with
studious politeness, but without uttering a word, before she settled herself in her chair. "I am obliged
to listen to this person," thought the old lady. "But
I am *not* obliged to speak to her. That is Julian's
business—not mine." "Don't stand, Horace! You
fidget me. Sit down." Armed beforehand in her
policy of silence, Lady Janet folded her handsome
hands as usual, and waited for the proceedings to
begin, like a judge on the bench.

"Will you take a chair?" Julian repeated, observing that the visitor appeared neither to heed nor to
hear his first words of welcome to her.

At this second appeal she spoke to him. "Is that
Lady Janet Roy?" she asked, with her eyes fixed on
the mistress of the house.

Julian answered, and drew back to watch the
result.

The woman in the poor black garments changed

her position for the first time. She moved slowly across the room to the place at which Lady Janet was sitting, and addressed her respectfully with perfect self-possession of manner. Her whole demeanour, from the moment when she had appeared at the door, had expressed—at once plainly and becomingly— confidence in the reception that awaited her.

· "Almost the last words my father said to me on his death-bed," she began, "were words, madam, which told me to expect protection and kindness from you."

It was not Lady Janet's business to speak. She listened with the blandest attention. She waited with the most exasperating silence, to hear more.

Grace Roseberry drew back a step—not intimidated —only mortified and surprised. "Was my father wrong?" she asked, with a simple dignity of tone and manner which forced Lady Janet to abandon her policy of silence, in spite of herself.

"Who was your father?" she asked, coldly.

Grace Roseberry answered the question in a tone of stern surprise.

"Has the servant not given you my card?" she said. "Don't you know my name?"

"Which of your names?" rejoined Lady Janet.

"I don't understand your ladyship."

"I will make myself understood. You asked me if I knew your name. I ask you, in return, which name it is? The name on your card is 'Miss Roseberry.' The name marked on your clothes, when you were in the hospital, was 'Mercy Merrick.'"

The self-possession which Grace had maintained from the moment when she had entered the dining-room, seemed now for the first time to be on the point of failing her. She turned and looked appealingly at Julian, who had thus far kept his place apart, listening attentively.

"Surely," she said, "your friend, the consul, has told you in his letter about the mark on the clothes?"

Something of the girlish hesitation and timidity which had marked her demeanour at her interview with Mercy in the French cottage, reappeared in her tone and manner as she spoke those words. The changes—mostly changes for the worse—wrought in her by the suffering through which she had passed since that time, were now (for the moment) effaced. All that was left of the better and simpler side of her character asserted itself in her brief appeal to Julian. She had hitherto repelled him. He began to feel a certain compassionate interest in her now.

"The consul has informed me of what you said to him," he answered kindly. "But, if you will take my advice, I recommend you to tell your story to Lady Janet in your own words."

Grace again addressed herself with submissive reluctance to Lady Janet.

"The clothes your ladyship speaks of," she said, "were the clothes of another woman. The rain was pouring when the soldiers detained me on the frontier. I had been exposed for hours to the weather—I was wet to the skin. The clothes marked 'Mercy Merrick' were the clothes lent to me by Mercy Merrick herself, while my own things were drying. I was struck by the shell in those clothes. I was carried away insensible in those clothes, after the operation had been performed on me."

Lady Janet listened to perfection—and did no more. She turned confidentially to Horace and said to him, in her gracefully ironical way, "She is ready with her explanation."

Horace answered in the same tone, "A great deal too ready."

Grace looked from one of them to the other. A faint flush of colour showed itself in her face for the first time.

"Am I to understand," she asked with proud composure, "that you don't believe me?"

Lady Janet maintained her policy of silence. She waved one hand courteously towards Julian, as if to say, "Address your inquiries to the gentleman who introduces you." Julian, noticing the gesture and observing the rising colour in Grace's cheeks, interfered directly in the interests of peace.

"Lady Janet asked you a question just now," he said; "Lady Janet inquired who your father was."

"My father was the late Colonel Roseberry."

Lady Janet looked indignantly at Horace. "Her assurance amazes me!" she exclaimed.

Julian interposed before his aunt could add a word more. "Pray let us hear her," he said in a tone of entreaty which had something of the imperative in it this time. He turned to Grace. "Have you any proof to produce," he added in his gentler voice, "which will satisfy us that you are Colonel Rose-, berry's daughter?"

Grace looked at him indignantly. "Proof!" she repeated. "Is my word not enough?"

Julian kept his temper perfectly. "Pardon me," he rejoined, "you forget that you and Lady Janet meet now for the first time. Try to put yourself in my aunt's place. How is she to know that you are the late Colonel Roseberry's daughter?"

Grace's head sank on her breast; she dropped into the nearest chair. The expression of her face changed instantly from anger to discouragement. "Ah," she exclaimed bitterly, "if I only had the letters that have been stolen from me!"

"Letters," asked Julian, "introducing you to Lady Janet?"

"Yes." She turned suddenly to Lady Janet. "Let me tell you how I lost them," she said, in the first tones of entreaty which had escaped her yet.

Lady Janet hesitated. It was not in her generous nature to resist the appeal that had just been made to her. The sympathies of Horace were far less easily reached. He lightly launched a new shaft of satire— intended for the private amusement of Lady Janet.

"Another explanation!" he exclaimed, with a sigh of comic resignation.

Julian overheard the words. His large lustrous eyes fixed themselves on Horace with a look of unmeasured contempt.

"The least you can do," he said, sternly, "is not to irritate her. It is so easy to irritate her!" He addressed himself again to Grace, endeavouring to help her through her difficulty in a new way. "Never mind explaining yourself for the moment," he said. "In the absence of your letters, have you any one in London who can speak to your identity?"

Grace shook her head sadly. "I have no friends in London," she answered.

It was impossible for Lady Janet—who had never in her life heard of anybody without friends in London —to pass this over without notice. "No friends in London!" she repeated, turning to Horace.

Horace shot another shaft of light satire. "Of course not!" he rejoined.

Grace saw them comparing notes. "My friends are in Canada," she broke out impetuously. "Plenty of friends who could speak for me, if I could only bring them here."

As a place of reference—mentioned in the capital city of England—Canada, there is no denying it, is open to objection on the ground of distance. Horace was ready with another shot. "Far enough off, certainly," he said.

"Far enough off, as you say," Lady Janet agreed.

Once more, Julian's inexhaustible kindness strove to obtain a hearing for the stranger who had been confided to his care. "A little patience, Lady Janet," he pleaded. "A little consideration, Horace, for a friendless woman."

"Thank you, sir," said Grace. "It is very kind of you to try and help me; but it is useless. They won't even listen to me." She attempted to rise from her chair as she pronounced the last words. Julian gently laid his hand on her shoulder and obliged her to resume her seat.

"*I* will listen to you," he said. "You referred me just now to the consul's letter. The consul tells me you suspected some one of taking your papers and your clothes."

"I don't suspect," was the quick reply, "I am

certain! I tell you positively Mercy Merrick was the
thief. She was alone with me when I was struck
down by the shell. She was the only person who
knew that I had letters of introduction about me.
She confessed to my face that she had been a bad
woman—she had been in a prison—she had come out
of a Refuge——"

Julian stopped her there with one plain question,
which threw a doubt on the whole story.

"The consul tells me you asked him to search for
Mercy Merrick," he said. "Is it not true that he
caused inquiries to be made, and that no trace of any
such person was to be heard of?"

"The consul took no pains to find her," Grace
answered angrily. "He was, like everybody else, in a
conspiracy to neglect and misjudge me."

Lady Janet and Horace exchanged looks. This
time it was impossible for Julian to blame them. The
farther the stranger's narrative advanced, the less
worthy of serious attention he felt it to be. The
longer she spoke, the more disadvantageously she
challenged comparison with the absent woman, whose
name she so obstinately and so audaciously persisted
in assuming as her own.

"Granting all that you have said," Julian resumed, with a last effort of patience, "what use could Mercy Merrick make of your letters and your clothes?"

"What use?" repeated Grace, amazed at his not seeing the position as she saw it. "My clothes were marked with my name. One of my papers was a letter from my father, introducing me to Lady Janet. A woman out of a Refuge would be quite capable of presenting herself here in my place."

Spoken entirely at random, spoken without so much as a fragment of evidence to support them, those last words still had their effect. They cast a reflection on Lady Janet's adopted daughter which was too outrageous to be borne. Lady Janet rose instantly. "Give me your arm, Horace," she said, turning to leave the room. "I have heard enough."

Horace respectfully offered his arm. "Your lady-ship is quite right," he answered. "A more monstrous story never was invented."

He spoke in the warmth of his indignation, loud enough for Grace to hear him. "What is there mon-strous in it?" she asked, advancing a step towards him defiantly.   .

Julian checked her. He too—though he had only

once seen Mercy—felt an angry sense of the insult offered to the beautiful creature who had interested him at his first sight of her. "Silence!" he said, speaking sternly to Grace for the first time. "You are offending—justly offending—Lady Janet. You are talking worse than absurdly—you are talking offensively —when you speak of another woman presenting herself here in your place."

Grace's blood was up. Stung by Julian's reproof, she turned on him a look which was almost a look of fury.

"Are you a clergyman? Are you an educated man?" she asked. "Have you never read of cases of false personation, in newspapers and books? I blindly confided in Mercy Merrick before I found out what her character really was. She left the cottage—I know it, from the surgeon who brought me to life again—firmly persuaded that the shell had killed me. My papers and my clothes disappeared at the same time. Is there nothing suspicious in these circumstances? There were people at the hospital who thought them highly suspicious—people who warned me that I might find an impostor in my place." She suddenly paused. The rustling sound of a silk dress

had caught her ear. Lady Janet was leaving the
room, with Horace, by way of the conservatory. With
a last desperate effort of resolution, Grace sprang forward, and placed herself in front of them.

"One word, Lady Janet, before you turn your back
on me," she said, firmly. "One word, and I will be
content. Has Colonel Roseberry's letter found its way
to this house or not? If it has, did a woman bring it
to you?"

Lady Janet looked—as only a great lady *can* look,
when a person of inferior rank has presumed to fail
in respect towards her.

"You are surely not aware," she said, with icy
composure, "that these questions are an insult to
Me?"

"And worse than an insult," Horace added warmly,
"to Grace!"

The little resolute black figure (still barring the
way to the conservatory) was suddenly shaken from
head to foot. The woman's eyes travelled backwards
and forwards between Lady Janet and Horace with
the light of a new suspicion in them.

"Grace!" she exclaimed. "What Grace? That's

my name. Lady Janet, you *have* got the letter! The woman is here!"

Lady Janet dropped Horace's arm, and retraced her steps to the place at which her nephew was standing.

"Julian," she said. "You force me for the first time in my life to remind you of the respect that is due to me in my own house. Send that woman away."

Without waiting to be answered, she turned back again, and once more took Horace's arm.

"Stand back, if you please," she said quietly to Grace.

Grace held her ground.

"The woman is here!" she repeated. "Confront me with her—and then send me away, if you like."

Julian advanced, and firmly took her by the arm. "You forget what is due to Lady Janet," he said, drawing her aside. "You forget what is due to yourself."

With a desperate effort, Grace broke away from him, and stopped Lady Janet on the threshold of the conservatory door.

"Justice!" she cried, shaking her clenched hand

with hysterical frenzy in the air. "I claim my right
to meet that woman face to face! Where is she?
Confront me with her! Confront me with her!"

: While those wild words were pouring from her
lips, the rumbling of carriage wheels became audible
on the drive in front of the house. In the all-absorb-
ing agitation of the moment, the sound of the wheels
(followed by the opening of the house door) passed
unnoticed by the persons in the dining-room. Horace's
voice was still raised in angry protest against the
insult offered to Lady Janet; Lady Janet herself
(leaving him for the second time) was vehemently
ringing the bell to summon the servants; Julian had
once more taken the infuriated woman by the arm,
and was trying vainly to compose her — when the
library door was opened quietly by a young lady
wearing a mantle and a bonnet. Mercy Merrick (true
to the appointment which she had made with Horace)
entered the room.

The first eyes that discovered her presence on the
scene were the eyes of Grace Roseberry. Starting
violently in Julian's grasp, she pointed towards the
library door. "Ah!" she cried, with a shriek of
vindictive delight. "There she is!"

Mercy turned as the sound of the scream rang through the room, and met—resting on her in savage triumph—the living gaze of the woman whose identity she had stolen, whose body she had left laid out for dead. On the instant of that terrible discovery—with her eyes fixed helplessly on the fierce eyes that had found her—she dropped senseless on the floor.

CHAPTER XII.

Exit Julian.

JULIAN happened to be standing nearest to Mercy.
He was the first at her side when she fell.

In the cry of alarm which burst from him, as he
raised her for a moment in his arms, in the expression
of his eyes when he looked at her death-like face,
there escaped the plain—too plain—confession of the
interest which he felt in her, of the admiration which
she had aroused in him. Horace detected it. There
was the quick suspicion of jealousy in the movement
by which he joined Julian; there was the ready resent-
ment of jealousy in the tone in which he pronounced
the words, "Leave her to me." Julian resigned her
in silence. A faint flush appeared on his pale face as
he drew back while Horace carried her to the sofa.
His eyes sank to the ground; he seemed to be medi-
tating self-reproachfully on the tone in which his
friend had spoken to him. After having been the
first to take an active part in meeting the calamity

that had happened, he was now to all appearance insensible to everything that was passing in the room.

A touch on his shoulder roused him.

He turned and looked round. The woman who had done the mischief—the stranger in the poor black garments—was standing behind him. She pointed to the prostrate figure on the sofa, with a merciless smile.

"You wanted a proof just now," she said. "There it is!"

Horace heard her. He suddenly left the sofa and joined Julian. His face, naturally ruddy, was pale with suppressed fury.

"Take that wretch away!" he said. "Instantly! or I won't answer for what I may do."

Those words recalled Julian to himself. He looked round the room. Lady Janet and the housekeeper were together, in attendance on the swooning woman. The startled servants were congregated in the library doorway. Mercy had endeared herself to them by many little acts of kindness and consideration. One of them offered to run to the nearest doctor. Another asked if he should fetch the police. A third—the servant who had been in attendance on Mercy when

the carriage took her to the committee-meeting—super-
stitiously assured Julian that it was Fate, and nothing
less, which had brought his young lady home exactly
at the wrong time. "They all disagreed at the meeting, sir," the man said; "and the chairman adjourned
the debate. If it hadn't been for that, we might not
have got back for another good hour to come."

With some difficulty, Julian quieted the anxiety
and confusion among the servants. This done, he
took Grace by the hand to lead her from the room.
She hesitated and tried to release herself. Julian
pointed to the group at the sofa, and to the servants
going out in a body by the library door. "You have
made an enemy of every one in this house," he said,
"and you have not a friend in London. Do you wish
to make an enemy of *me?*" Her head drooped; she
made no reply; she waited, dumbly obedient to the
firmer will than her own. Julian withdrew to the
library, leading Grace after him by the hand. Before
closing the door he paused, and looked back into the
dining-room.

"Is she recovering?" he asked, after a moment's
hesitation.

Lady Janet's voice answered him. "Not yet."

"Shall I send for the nearest doctor?"

Horace interposed. He declined to let Julian associate himself, even in that indirect manner, with Mercy's recovery.

"If the doctor is wanted," he said, "I will go for him myself."

Julian closed the library door. He absently released Grace; he mechanically pointed to a chair. She sat down in silent surprise, following him with her eyes as he walked slowly to and fro in the room.

For the moment his mind was far away from her, and from all that had happened since her appearance in the house. It was impossible that a man of his fineness of perception could mistake the meaning of Horace's conduct towards him. He was questioning his own heart, on the subject of Mercy, sternly and unreservedly as it was his habit to do. "After only once seeing her," he thought, "has she produced such an impression on me that Horace can discover it, before I have even suspected it myself? Can the time have come already, when I owe it to my friend to see her no more?" He stopped irritably in his walk. As a man devoted to a serious calling in life, there was something that wounded his self-respect in the bare

suspicion that he could be guilty of the purely senti-
mental extravagance called "love at first sight."

He had paused exactly opposite to the chair in
which Grace was seated. Weary of the silence, she
seized the opportunity of speaking to him.

"I have come here with you as you wished," she
said. "Are you going to help me? Am I to count
on you as my friend?"

He looked at her vacantly. It cost him an effort
before he could give her the attention that she had
claimed.

"You have been hard on me," Grace went on.
"But you showed me some kindness at first; you tried
to make them give me a fair hearing. I ask you, as
a just man, do you doubt now that the woman on
the sofa in the next room is an impostor who has
taken my place? Can there be any plainer confession
that she is Mercy Merrick than the confession she has
made? *You* saw it; *they* saw it. She fainted at the
sight of me."

Julian crossed the room — still without answering
her—and rang the bell. When the servant appeared,
he told the man to fetch a cab.

Grace rose from her chair. "What is the cab for?" she asked sharply.

"For you and for me," Julian replied. "I am going to take you back to your lodgings."

"I refuse to go. My place is in this house. Neither Lady Janet nor you can get over the plain facts. All I asked was to be confronted with her. And what, did she do when she came into the room. She fainted at the sight of me."

Reiterating her one triumphant assertion, she fixed her eyes on Julian with a look which said plainly, Answer that if you can. In mercy to *her*, Julian answered it on the spot.

"So far as I understand," he said, "you appear to take it for granted that no innocent woman would have fainted on first seeing you. I have something to tell you which will alter your opinion. On her arrival in England this lady informed my aunt that she had met with you accidentally on the French frontier, and that she had seen you (so far as she knew) struck dead at her side by a shell. Remember that, and recall what happened just now. Without a word to warn her of your restoration to life, she finds herself suddenly face to face with you, a living woman

—and this at a time when it is easy for any one who looks at her to see that she is in delicate health. What is there wonderful, what is there unaccountable, in her fainting under such circumstances as these?"

The question was plainly put. Where was the answer to it?

There was no answer to it. Mercy's wisely candid statement of the manner in which she had first met with Grace, and of the accident which had followed, had served Mercy's purpose but too well. It was simply impossible for persons acquainted with that statement to attach a guilty meaning to the swoon. The false Grace Roseberry was still as far beyond the reach of suspicion as ever; and the true Grace was quick enough to see it. She sank into the chair from which she had risen; her hands fell in hopeless despair on her lap.

"Everything is against me," she said. "The truth itself turns liar, and takes *her* side." She paused and rallied her sinking courage. "No!" she cried resolutely, "I won't submit to have my name and my place taken from me by a vile adventuress! Say what you like, I insist on exposing her; I won't leave the house!"

The servant entered the room, and announced that the cab was at the door.

Grace turned to Julian with a defiant wave of her hand. "Don't let me detain you," she said. "I see I have neither advice nor help to expect from Mr. Julian Gray."

Julian beckoned to the servant to follow him into a corner of the room.

"Do you know if the doctor has been sent for?" he asked.

"I believe not, sir. It is said in the servants' hall that the doctor is not wanted."

Julian was too anxious to be satisfied with a report from the servants' hall. He hastily wrote on a slip of paper: "Has she recovered?" and then gave the note to the man, with directions to take it to Lady Janet.

"Did you hear what I said?" Grace inquired, while the messenger was absent in the dining-room.

"I will answer you directly," said Julian.

The servant appeared again as he spoke, with some lines in pencil written by Lady Janet on the back of Julian's note. "Thank God we have revived

her. In a few minutes we hope to be able to take
her to her room."

The nearest way to Mercy's room was through the
library. Grace's immediate removal had now become
a necessity which was not to be trifled with. Julian
addressed himself to meeting the difficulty the instant
he was left alone with Grace.

"Listen to me," he said. "The cab is waiting, and
I have my last words to say to you. You are now
(thanks to the consul's recommendation) in my care.
Decide at once whether you will remain under my
charge, or whether you will transfer yourself to the
charge of the police."

Grace started. "What do you mean?" she asked
angrily.

"If you wish to remain under my charge," Julian
proceeded, "you will accompany me at once to the
cab. In that case I will undertake to give you an opportunity of telling your story to my own lawyer. He
will be a fitter person to advise you than I am. Nothing will induce *me* to believe that the lady whom
you have accused has committed, or is capable of
committing, such a fraud as you charge her with. You
will hear what the lawyer thinks, if you come with me.

If you refuse, I shall have no choice but to send into
the next room and tell them that you are still here.
The result will be that you will find yourself in charge
of the police. Take which course you like; I will give
you a minute to decide in. And remember this, if
I appear to express myself harshly, it is your conduct
which forces me to speak out. I mean kindly towards
you; I am advising you honestly for your good."

He took out his watch to count the minute.

Grace stole one furtive glance at his steady resolute face. She was perfectly unmoved by the manly
consideration for her which Julian's last words had expressed. All she understood was, that he was not a
man to be trifled with. Future opportunities would
offer themselves of returning secretly to the house.
She determined to yield—and deceive him.

"I am ready to go," she said, rising with dogged
submission. "Your turn now," she muttered to herself
as she turned to the looking glass to arrange her
shawl. "My turn will come."

Julian advanced towards her, as if to offer her his
arm, and checked himself. Firmly persuaded as he
was that her mind was deranged—readily as he admitted that she claimed, in virtue of her affliction,

every indulgence that he could extend to her—there
was something repellant to him at that moment in the
bare idea of touching her. The image of the beautiful
creature who was the object of her monstrous accusa-
tion—the image of Mercy as she lay helpless for a
moment in his arms—was vivid in his mind while he
opened the door that led into the hall, and drew back
to let Grace pass out before him. He left the servant
to help her into the cab. The man respectfully addressed him as he took his seat opposite to Grace.

"I am ordered to say that your room is ready, sir;
and that her ladyship expects you to dinner."

Absorbed in the events which had followed his
aunt's invitation, Julian had forgotten his engagement
to stay at Mablethorpe House. Could he return,
knowing his own heart as he now knew it? Could he
honourably remain, perhaps for weeks together, in
Mercy's society, conscious as he now was of the impression which she had produced on him? No. The
one honourable course that he could take was to find
an excuse for withdrawing from his engagement. "Beg
her ladyship not to wait dinner for me," he said. "I
will write and make my apologies." The cab drove
off. The wondering servant waited on the doorstep,

looking after it. "I wouldn't stand in Mr. Julian's shoes for something," he thought, with his mind running on the difficulties of the young clergyman's position. "There she is, along with him in the cab. What is he going to do with her after that?"

Julian himself—if it had been put to him at the moment—could not have answered the question.

Lady Janet's anxiety was far from being relieved when Mercy had been restored to her senses and conducted to her own room.

Her mind remained in a condition of unreasoning alarm which it was impossible to remove. Over and over again, she was told that the woman who had terrified her had left the house, and would never be permitted to enter it more. Over and over again, she was assured that the stranger's frantic assertions were regarded by everybody about her as unworthy of a moment's serious attention. She persisted in doubting whether they were telling her the truth. A shocking distrust of her friends seemed to possess her. She shrank when Lady Janet approached the bedside. She shuddered when Lady Janet kissed her. She flatly refused to let Horace see her. She asked the strangest

questions about Julian Gray, and shook her head
suspiciously when they told her that he was absent
from the house. At intervals, she hid her face in the
bedclothes, and murmured to herself piteously. "Oh!
what shall I do? What shall I do?" At other times,
her one petition was to be left alone. "I want nobody
in my room"—that was her sullen cry—"Nobody in
my room!"

The evening advanced, and brought with it no
change for the better. Lady Janet, by the advice of
Horace, sent for her own medical adviser.

The doctor shook his head. The symptoms, he
said, indicated a serious shock to the nervous system.
He wrote a sedative prescription; and he gave (with
a happy choice of language) some sound and safe advice. It amounted briefly to this: "Take her away,
and try the sea-side." Lady Janet's customary energy
acted on the advice without a moment's needless delay. She gave the necessary directions for packing
the trunks over night, and decided on leaving Mablethorpe House with Mercy the next morning.

Shortly after the doctor had taken his departure,
a letter from Julian, addressed to Lady Janet, was de-
livered by private messenger.

Beginning with the necessary apologies for the writer's absence, the letter proceeded in these terms:

"Before I permitted my companion to accompany me to the lawyer's office, I felt the necessity of consulting him as to my present position towards her.

"I told him—what I think it only right to repeat to you—that I do not feel justified in acting on my own opinion that her mind is deranged. In the case of this friendless woman, I want medical authority, and, more even than that, I want some positive proof, to satisfy my conscience as well as to confirm my view.

"Finding me obstinate on this point, the lawyer undertook to consult a physician accustomed to the treatment of the insane, on my behalf.

"After sending a message, and receiving the answer, he said, 'Bring the lady here—in half an hour; she shall tell her story to the doctor instead of telling it to me.' The proposal rather staggered me; I asked how it was possible to induce her to do that. He laughed, and answered, 'I shall present the doctor as my senior partner; my senior partner will be the very man to advise her.' You know that I hate all decep-

13*

tion—even where the end in view appears to justify it. On this occasion, however, there was no other alternative than to let the lawyer take his own course— or to run the risk of a delay which might be followed by serious results.

"I waited in a room by myself (feeling very uneasy I own) until the doctor joined me after the interview was over.

"His opinion is, briefly, this:

"After careful examination of the unfortunate creature, he thinks that there are unmistakably symptoms of mental aberration. But how far the mischief has gone, and whether her case is, or is not, sufficiently grave to render actual restraint necessary, he cannot positively say, in our present state of ignorance as to facts.

"'Thus far,' he observed, 'we know nothing of that part of her delusion which relates to Mercy Merrick. The solution of the difficulty, in this case, is to be found there. I entirely agree with the lady that the enquiries of the consul at Mannheim are far from being conclusive. Furnish me with satisfactory evidence either that there is, or is not, such a person really in existence as Mercy Merrick, and I will give you a

positive opinion on the case, whenever you choose to
ask for it.'

"Those words have decided me on starting for
the Continent, and renewing the search for the missing
nurse.

"My friend the lawyer wonders jocosely whether *I*
am in my right senses. His advice is, that I should
apply to the nearest magistrate, and relieve you and
myself of all further trouble in that way.

"Perhaps you agree with him? My dear aunt (as
you have often said) I do nothing like other people.
I am interested in this case. I cannot abandon a forlorn woman who has been confided to me to the
tender mercies of strangers, so long as there is any
hope of my making discoveries which may be in-
strumental in restoring her to herself—perhaps, also,
in restoring her to her friends.

"I start by the mail train of to-night. My plan is,
to go first to Mannheim, and consult with the consul
and the hospital doctors; then to find my way to the
German surgeon, and to question *him;* and, that
done, to make the last and hardest effort of all—the
effort to trace the French ambulance and to penetrate
the mystery of Mercy Merrick.

"Immediately on my return I will wait on you, and tell you what I have accomplished, or how I have failed.

"In the meanwhile, pray be under no alarm about the reappearance of this unhappy woman at your house. She is fully occupied in writing (at my suggestion) to her friends in Canada; and she is under the care of the landlady at her lodgings—an experienced and trustworthy person, who has satisfied the doctor as well as myself of her fitness for the charge that she has undertaken.

"Pray mention this to Miss Roseberry (whenever you think it desirable), with the respectful expression of my sympathy, and of my best wishes for her speedy restoration to health. And once more forgive me for failing, under stress of necessity, to enjoy the hospitality of Mablethorpe House."

Lady Janet closed Julian's letter, feeling far from satisfied with it. She sat for a while, pondering over what her nephew had written to her.

"One of two things," thought the quick-witted old lady. "Either the lawyer is right, and Julian is a fit companion for the madwoman whom he has taken

under his charge: or he has some second motive for
this absurd journey of his, which he has carefully abstained from mentioning in his letter. What can the
motive be?"

At intervals during the night, that question re-
curred to her ladyship again and again. The utmost
exercise of her ingenuity failing to answer it, her one
resource left was to wait patiently for Julian's return,
and, in her own favourite phrase, to "have it out with
him" then.

The next morning, Lady Janet and her adopted
daughter left Mablethorpe House for Brighton; Horace
(who had begged to be allowed to accompany them)
being sentenced to remain in London by Mercy's express desire. Why—nobody could guess; and Mercy
refused to say.

CHAPTER XIII.

Enter Julian.

A WEEK has passed. The scene opens again in
the dining-room at Mablethorpe House.

The hospitable table bears once more its burden
of good things for lunch. But, on this occasion, Lady
Janet sits alone. Her attention is divided between
reading her newspaper and feeding her cat. The cat
is a sleek and splendid creature. He carries an erect
tail. He rolls luxuriously on the soft carpet. He
approaches his mistress in a series of coquettish
curves. He smells with dainty hesitation at the choicest
morsels that can be offered to him. The musical
monotony of his purring falls soothingly on her ladyship's ear. She stops in the middle of a leading
article, and looks with a careworn face at the happy
cat. "Upon my honour," cries Lady Janet, thinking,
in her inveterately ironical manner, of the cares that
trouble her, "all things considered, Tom, I wish I was
You!"

The cat starts—not at his mistress's complimentary
apostrophe, but at a knock at the door which follows

close upon it. Lady Janet says, carelessly enough, "Come in;" looks round listlessly to see who it is; and starts, like the cat, when the door opens and discloses—Julian Gray!

"You—or your ghost?" she exclaims.

She has noticed already that Julian is paler than usual, and that there is something in his manner at once uneasy and subdued—highly uncharacteristic of him at other times. He takes a seat by her side, and kisses her hand. But—for the first time in his aunt's experience of him—he refuses the good things on the luncheon-table, and he has nothing to say to the cat! That neglected animal takes refuge on Lady Janet's lap. Lady Janet, with her eyes fixed expectantly on her nephew (determining to "have it out with him," at the first opportunity) waits to hear what he has to say for himself. Julian has no alternative but to break the silence, and tell his story as he best may.

"I got back from the Continent last night," he began. "And I come here, as I promised, to report myself on my return. How does your ladyship do? How is Miss Roseberry?"

Lady Janet laid an indicative finger on the lace pelerine which ornamented the upper part of her dress. "Here is the old lady, well," she answered—and pointed next to the room above them. "And there," she added, "is the young lady, ill. Is anything the matter with *you*, Julian?"

"Perhaps I am a little tired after my journey. Never mind me. Is Miss Roseberry still suffering from the shock?"

"What else should she be suffering from? I will never forgive you, Julian, for bringing that crazy impostor into my house."

"My dear aunt, when I was the innocent means of bringing her here I had no idea that such a person as Miss Roseberry was in existence. Nobody laments what has happened more sincerely than I do. Have you had medical advice?"

"I took her to the sea-side a week since, by medical advice."

"Has the change of air done her no good?"

"None whatever. If anything, the change of air has made her worse. Sometimes she sits for hours together, as pale as death, without looking at anything, and without uttering a word. Sometimes she

brightens up, and seems as if she was eager to say
something—and then, Heaven only knows why, checks
herself suddenly as if she was afraid to speak. I
could support that. But what cuts me to the heart,
Julian, is, that she does not appear to trust me and
to love me as she did. She seems to be doubtful of
me; she seems to be frightened of me. If I did not
know that it was simply impossible that such a thing
could be, I should really think she suspected me of
believing what that wretch said of her. In one word
(and between ourselves) I begin to fear she will never
get over the fright which caused that fainting fit.
There is serious mischief somewhere—and try as I
may to discover it, it is mischief beyond my finding."

"Can the doctor do nothing?"

Lady Janet's bright black eyes answered, before
she replied in words, with a look of supreme contempt.

"The doctor!" she repeated disdainfully. "I
brought Grace back last night in sheer despair, and I
sent for the doctor this morning. He is at the head
of his profession; he is said to be making ten thousand a year—and he knows no more about it than I
do. I am quite serious. The great physician has

just gone away with two guineas in his pocket. One
guinea for advising me to keep her quiet; another
guinea for telling me to trust to time. Do you wonder
how he gets on at this rate? My dear boy, they all
get on in the same way. The medical profession
thrives on two incurable diseases in these modern
days—a He-disease and a She-disease. She-disease—
nervous depression; He-disease — suppressed gout.
Remedies, one guinea if *you* go to the doctor; two
guineas if the doctor goes to *you*. I might have
bought a new bonnet," cried her ladyship indignantly,
"with the money I have given to that man! Let us
change the subject. I lose my temper when I think
of it. Besides, I want to know something. Why did
you go abroad?"

At that plain question Julian looked unaffectedly
surprised. "I wrote to explain," he said. "Have you
not received my letter?"

"Oh, I got your letter. It was long enough, in all
conscience—and, long as it was, it didn't tell me the
one thing I wanted to know."

"What is the 'one thing?'"

Lady Janet's reply pointed—not too palpably at

first—at that second motive for Julian's journey which she had suspected Julian of concealing from her.

"I want to know," she said, "why you troubled yourself to make your enquiries on the Continent *in person?* You know where my old courier is to be found. You have yourself pronounced him to be the most intelligent and trustworthy of men. Answer me honestly—could you not have sent him in your place?"

"I *might* have sent him," Julian admitted—a little reluctantly.

"You might have sent the courier—and you were under an engagement to stay here as my guest. Answer me honestly once more. Why did you go away?"

Julian hesitated. Lady Janet paused for his reply, with the air of a woman who was prepared to wait (if necessary) for the rest of the afternoon.

"I had a reason of my own for going," Julian said at last.

"Yes?" rejoined Lady Janet, prepared to wait (if necessary) till the next morning.

"A reason," Julian resumed, "which I would rather not mention."

"Oh!" said Lady Janet. "Another mystery—eh? And another woman at the bottom of it, no doubt? Thank you—that will do—I am sufficiently answered. No wonder—as a clergyman—that you look a little confused. There is perhaps a certain grace, under the circumstances, in looking confused. We will change the subject again. You stay here, of course, now you have come back?"

Once more the famous pulpit orator seemed to find himself in the inconceivable predicament of not knowing what to say. Once more Lady Janet looked resigned to wait—(if necessary) until the middle of next week.

Julian took refuge in an answer worthy of the most commonplace man on the face of the civilised earth.

"I beg your ladyship to accept my thanks and my excuses," he said.

Lady Janet's many-ringed fingers mechanically stroking the cat in her lap, began to stroke him the wrong way. Lady Janet's inexhaustible patience showed signs of failing her at last.

"Mighty civil, I am sure," she said. "Make it complete. Say, Mr. Julian Gray presents his compliments to Lady Janet Roy, and regrets that a previous engagement—Julian!" exclaimed the old lady, suddenly pushing the cat off her lap, and flinging her last pretence of good temper to the winds—"Julian, I am not to be trifled with! There is but one explanation of your conduct—you are evidently avoiding my house. Is there somebody you dislike in it? Is it me?"

Julian intimated by a gesture that his aunt's last question was absurd. (The much-injured cat elevated his back, waved his tail slowly, walked to the fireplace, and honoured the rug by taking a seat on it.)

Lady Janet persisted. "Is it Grace Roseberry?" she asked next.

Even Julian's patience began to show signs of yielding. His manner assumed a sudden decision, his voice rose a tone louder.

"You insist on knowing?" he said. "It *is* Miss Roseberry."

"You don't like her?" cried Lady Janet, with a sudden burst of angry surprise.

Julian broke out, on his side. "If I see any more of her," he answered, the rare colour mounting suddenly in his cheeks, "I shall be the unhappiest man living. If I see any more of her, I shall be false to my old friend who is to marry her. Keep us apart. If you have any regard for my peace of mind, keep us apart."

Unutterable amazement expressed itself in his aunt's lifted hands. Ungovernable curiosity uttered itself in his aunt's next words.

"You don't mean to tell me you are in love with Grace?"

Julian sprang restlessly to his feet, and disturbed the cat at the fireplace. (The cat left the room.)

"I don't know what to tell you," he said, "I can't realise it to myself. No other woman has ever roused the feeling in me which *this* woman seems to have called to life in an instant. In the hope of forgetting her I broke my engagement here; I purposely seized the opportunity of making those inquiries abroad. Quite useless. I think of her morning, noon, and night. I see her and hear her, at this moment, as plainly as I see and hear You. She has made *her*-self a part of *my*-self. I don't understand my life without her. My power of will seems to be gone. I said to myself this morning, 'I will write to my aunt; I won't go back to Mablethorpe House.' Here I am in Mablethorpe House, with a mean subterfuge to justify me to my own conscience. 'I owe it to my aunt to call on my aunt.' That is what I said to myself on the way here; and I was secretly hoping every step of the way that She would come into the room when I got here. I am hoping it now. And she is engaged to Horace Holmcroft—to my oldest friend, to my best friend! Am I an infernal rascal? or am I a weak fool? God knows—I don't. Keep my secret, aunt. I am heartily ashamed of myself: I used to think I was made of better stuff than this. Don't say a word to Horace. I must, and will, conquer it. Let me go."

He snatched up his hat. Lady Janet, rising with the activity of a young woman, pursued him across the room, and stopped him at the door.

"No," answered the resolute old lady, "I won't let you go. Come back with me."

As she said those words she noticed with a certain fond pride the brilliant colour mounting in his cheeks —the flashing brightness which lent an added lustre to his eyes. He had never, to her mind, looked so handsome before. She took his arm, and led him to the chairs which they had just left. It was shocking,

it was wrong (she mentally admitted), to look on
Mercy, under the circumstances, with any other eye
than the eye of a brother or a friend. In a clergyman
(perhaps) doubly shocking, doubly wrong. But, with
all her respect for the vested interests of Horace,
Lady Janet could not blame Julian. Worse still, she
was privately conscious that he had, somehow or
other, risen, rather than fallen, in her estimation
within the last minute or two. Who could deny that
her adopted daughter was a charming creature? Who
could wonder if a man of refined tastes admired her?
Upon the whole, her ladyship humanely decided that
her nephew was rather to be pitied than blamed.
What daughter of Eve (no matter whether she was
seventeen or seventy) could have honestly arrived at
any other conclusion? Do what a man may—let him
commit anything he likes, from an error to a crime—
so long as there is a woman at the bottom of it, there
is an inexhaustible fund of pardon for him in every
other woman's heart. "Sit down," said Lady Janet,
smiling in spite of herself; "and don't talk in that
horrible way again. A man, Julian—especially a
famous man like you—ought to know how to control
himself."

Julian burst out laughing bitterly.

"Send upstairs for my self-control," he said. "It's in *her* possession—not in mine. Good morning, aunt."

He rose from his chair. Lady Janet instantly pushed him back into it.

"I insist on your staying here," she said, "if it's only for a few minutes longer. I have something to say to you."

"Does it refer to Miss Roseberry?"

"It refers to the hateful woman who frightened Miss Roseberry. Now are you satisfied?"

Julian bowed, and settled himself in his chair.

"I don't much like to acknowledge it," his aunt went on. "But I want you to understand that I have something really serious to speak about, for once in a way. Julian! that wretch not only frightens Grace—she actually frightens Me."

"Frightens you? She is quite harmless, poor thing."

"'Poor thing!'" repeated Lady Janet. "Did you say 'poor thing?'"

"Yes."

"Is it possible that you pity her?"

14*

"From the bottom of my heart."

The old lady's temper gave way again at that reply. "I hate a man who can't hate anybody!" she burst out. "If you had been an ancient Roman, Julian, I believe you would have pitied Nero himself."

Julian cordially agreed with her. "I believe I should," he said quietly. "All sinners, my dear aunt, are more or less miserable sinners. Nero must have been one of the wretchedest of mankind."

"Wretched!" exclaimed Lady Janet. "Nero wretched! A man who committed robbery, arson, and murder, to his own violin accompaniment—*only* wretched! What next, I wonder? When modern philanthropy begins to apologise . for Nero,* modern philanthropy has arrived at a pretty pass indeed! We shall hear next that Bloody Queen Mary was as playful as a kitten; and if poor dear Henry the Eighth carried anything to an extreme, it was the practice of the domestic virtues. Ah, how I hate cant! What were we talking about just now? You wander from the subject, Julian; you are, what I call, bird-witted. I protest I forget what I wanted to say to you. No, I won't be reminded of it. I may be an old woman, but I am not in my dotage yet! Why do you sit there staring? Have you nothing to say for yourself? Of all the people in the world, have *you* lost the use of your tongue?"

Julian's excellent temper and accurate knowledge of his aunt's character, exactly fitted him to calm the rising storm. He contrived to lead Lady Janet insensibly back to the lost subject, by dexterous reference to a narrative which he had thus far left untold—the narrative of his adventures on the Continent.

"I have a great deal to say, aunt," he replied. "I have not yet told you of my discoveries abroad."

Lady Janet instantly took the bait.

"I knew there was something forgotten," she said. "You have been all this time in the house, and you have told me nothing. Begin directly."

Patient Julian began.

CHAPTER XIV.

Coming Events cast their Shadows before.

"I WENT first to Mannheim, Lady Janet, as I told
you I should in my letter; and I heard all that the
consul and the hospital doctors could tell me. No
new fact of the slightest importance turned up. I got
my directions for finding the German surgeon, and I
set forth to try what I could make next of the man
who had performed the operation. On the question
of his patient's identity he had (as a perfect stranger
to her) nothing to tell me. On the question of her
mental condition, however, he made a very important
statement He owned to me that he had operated
on another person injured by a shell-wound on the
head, at the battle of Solferino, and that the patient
(recovering also in this case) recovered—mad. That
is a remarkable admission; don't you think so?"

Lady Janet's temper had hardly been allowed time
enough to subside to its customary level.

"Very remarkable, I dare say," she answered, "to
people who feel any doubt of this pitiable lady of

yours being mad. I feel no doubt—and, thus far, I find your account of yourself, Julian, tiresome in the extreme. Get on to the end. Did you lay your hand on Mercy Merrick?"

"No."

"Did you hear anything of her?"

"Nothing. Difficulties beset me on every side. The French ambulance had shared in the disasters of France—it was broken up. The wounded Frenchmen were prisoners, somewhere in Germany, nobody knew where. The French surgeon had been killed in action. His assistants were scattered—most likely in hiding. I began to despair of making any discovery, when accident threw in my way two Prussian soldiers who had been in the French cottage. They confirmed what the German surgeon told the consul, and what Horace himself told *me*, namely, that no nurse in a black dress was to be seen in the place. If there had been such a person, she would certainly (the Prussians informed me) have been found in attendance on the injured Frenchmen. The cross of the Geneva Convention would have been amply sufficient to protect her: no woman wearing that badge of honour would have disgraced herself by abandoning the wounded men before the Germans entered the place."

"In short," interposed Lady Janet, "there is no such person as Mercy Merrick?"

"I can draw no other conclusion," said Julian, "unless the English doctor's idea is the right one. After hearing what I have just told you, he is satisfied that the woman herself is Mercy Merrick."

Lady Janet held up her hand, as a sign that she had an objection to make here.

"You and the doctor seem to have settled everything to your entire satisfaction on both sides," she said. "But there is one difficulty that you have neither of you accounted for yet."

"What is it, aunt?"

"You talk glibly enough, Julian, about this woman's mad assertion that Grace is the missing nurse, and that she is Grace. But you have not explained yet how the idea first got into her head; and, more than that, how it is that she is acquainted with my name and address, and perfectly familiar with Grace's papers and Grace's affairs. These things are a puzzle to a person of my average intelligence. Can your clever friend, the doctor, account for them?"

"Shall I tell you what he said when I saw him this morning?"

"Will it take long?"

"It will take about a minute."

"You agreeably surprise me. Go on."

"You want to know how she gained her knowledge of your name, and of Miss Roseberry's affairs," Julian resumed. "The doctor says, in one of two ways. Either Miss Roseberry must have spoken of you, and of her own affairs, while she and the stranger were together in the French cottage; or the stranger must have obtained access privately to Miss Roseberry's papers. Do you agree so far?"

Lady Janet began to feel interested for the first time.

"Perfectly," she said. "I have no doubt Grace produced a strong impression on her, in the first place. I dare say all sorts of inquisitive questions followed; and Grace rashly talked of matters which an older and wiser person would have kept to herself."

"Very good. Do you also agree that the last idea in the woman's mind when she was struck by the shell, might have been (quite probably) the idea of

Miss Roseberry's identity and Miss Roseberry's affairs? You think it likely enough? Well! what happens after that? The wounded woman is brought to life by an operation, and she becomes delirious in the hospital at Mannheim. During her delirium the idea of Miss Roseberry's identity ferments in her brain, and assumes its present perverted form. In that form, it still remains. As a necessary consequence, she persists in reversing the two identities. She says she is Miss Roseberry, and declares Miss Roseberry to be Mercy Merrick. There is the doctor's view of the matter. As I think, it not only answers your question—it also explains the woman's angry repudiation of the name marked on her clothes (the name of Mercy Merrick) when she was received at the hospital. Do you agree with me?"

"I hardly know, Julian, whether I agree with you or not. Confusion of their own identity with the identity of others is common enough among mad people, I admit. Still, the doctor doesn't quite satisfy me. I think——"

What Lady Janet thought was not destined to be expressed. She suddenly checked herself, and held up her hand for the second time.

"Another objection?" inquired Julian.

"Hold your tongue!" cried the old lady. "If you say a word more I shall lose it again."

"Lose what, aunt?"

"What I wanted to say to you, ages ago. I have got it back again—it begins with a question. (No more of the doctor! I have had enough of him!) Where is she—*your* pitiable lady, *my* crazy wretch— where is she now? Still in London?"

"Yes."

"And still at large?"

"Still with the landlady, at her lodgings."

"Very well. Now, answer me this. What is to prevent her from making another attempt to force her way (or steal her way) into my house? How am I to protect Grace, how am I to protect myself, if she comes here again?"

"Is that really what you wished to speak to me about?"

"That, and nothing else."

They were both too deeply interested in the subject of their conversation to look towards the conservatory, and to notice the appearance at that mo-

ment of a distant gentleman among the plants and
flowers, who had made his way in from the garden
outside.   Advancing noiselessly on the soft Indian
matting, the gentleman ere long revealed himself under
the form and features of Horace Holmcroft.   Before
entering the dining-room, he paused, fixing his eyes
inquisitively on the back of Lady Janet's visitor—the
back being all that he could see in the position he
then occupied. After a pause of an instant, the visitor
spoke, and further uncertainty was at once at an
end.   Horace, nevertheless, made no movement to
enter the room.   He had his own jealous distrust
of what Julian might be tempted to confess privately
to Lady Janet; and he waited a little longer, on the
chance that his doubts might be verified.

"Neither you nor Miss Roseberry need any protection from the poor deluded creature," Julian went
on.   "I have gained great influence over her—and I
have satisfied her that it is useless to present herself
here again."

"I beg your pardon," interposed Horace, speaking
from the conservatory door. "You have done nothing
of the sort."

(He had heard enough to satisfy him that the

talk was not taking the direction which his suspicions had anticipated. And, as an additional incentive to show himself, a happy chance had now offered him the opportunity of putting Julian in the wrong.)

"Good heavens, Horace!" exclaimed Lady Janet, "where do you come from? And what do you mean?"

"I heard at the lodge that your ladyship and Grace had returned last night. And I came in at once, without troubling the servants, by the shortest way." He turned to Julian next. "The woman you were speaking of just now," he proceeded, "has been here again already—in Lady Janet's absence."

Lady Janet immediately looked at her nephew. Julian reassured her by a gesture.

"Impossible," he said. "There must be some mistake."

"There is no mistake," Horace rejoined. "I am repeating what I have just heard from the lodge-keeper himself. He hesitated to mention it to Lady Janet for fear of alarming her. Only three days since, this person had the audacity to ask him for her ladyship's address at the sea-side. Of course he refused to give it."

"You hear that, Julian?" said Lady Janet.

No signs of anger or mortification escaped Julian. The expression in his face at that moment was an expression of sincere distress.

"Pray don't alarm yourself," he said to his aunt, in his quietest tones. "If she attempts to annoy you or Miss Roseberry again, I have it in my power to stop her instantly."

"How?" asked Lady Janet.

"How, indeed!" echoed Horace. "If we give her in charge to the police we shall become the subject of a public scandal."

"I have managed to avoid all danger of scandal," Julian answered; the expression of distress in his face becoming more and more marked while he spoke. "Before I called here to-day I had a private consultation with the magistrate of the district, and I have made certain arrangements at the police-station close by. On receipt of my card, an experienced man, in plain clothes, will present himself at any address that I indicate, and will take her quietly away. The magistrate will hear the charge in his private room, and will examine the evidence which I can produce, showing that she is not accountable for her actions.

The proper medical officer will report officially on the case, and the law will place her under the necessary restraint."

Lady Janet and Horace looked at each other in amazement. Julian was, in their opinion, the last man on earth to take the course—at once sensible and severe—which Julian had actually adopted. Lady Janet insisted on an explanation.

"Why do I hear of this now for the first time?" she asked. "Why did you not tell me you had taken these precautions before?"

Julian answered frankly and sadly.

"Because I hoped, aunt, that there would be no necessity for proceeding to extremities. You now force me to acknowledge that the lawyer and the doctor (both of whom I have seen this morning) think, as you do, that she is not to be trusted. It was at their suggestion entirely that I went to the magistrate. They put it to me whether the result of my inquiries abroad—unsatisfactory as it may have been in other respects—did not strengthen the conclusion that the poor woman's mind is deranged. I felt compelled in common honesty to admit that it was so. Having owned this, I was bound to take such precautions as

the lawyer and the doctor thought necessary. I have
done my duty—sorely against my own will. It is
weak of me, I daresay—but I can *not* bear the thought
of treating this afflicted creature harshly. Her delusion is so hopeless! her situation is such a pitiable
one!"

His voice faltered. He turned away abruptly and
took up his hat. Lady Janet followed him, and spoke
to him at the door. Horace smiled satirically, and
went to warm himself at the fire.

"Are you going away, Julian?"

"I am only going to the lodge-keeper. I want to
give him a word of warning in case of his seeing her
again."

"You will come back here?" (Lady Janet lowered
her voice to a whisper). "There is really a reason,
Julian, for your not leaving the house now."

"I promise not to go away, aunt, until I have
provided for your security. If you, or your adopted
daughter, are alarmed by another intrusion, I give
you my word of honour my card shall go to the
police-station—however painfully I may feel it myself." (He, too, lowered his voice at the next words.)
"In the meantime, remember what I confessed to you

while we were alone! For my sake, let me see as little of Miss Roseberry as possible. Shall I find you in this room when I come back?"

"Yes."

"Alone?"

He laid a strong emphasis, of look as well as of tone, on that one word. Lady Janet understood what the emphasis meant.

"Are you really," she whispered, "as much in love with Grace as that?"

Julian laid one hand on his aunt's arm, and pointed with the other to Horace—standing with his back to them, warming his feet on the fender.

"Well?" said Lady Janet.

"Well," said Julian, with a smile on his lip and a tear in his eye, "I never envied any man as I envy *him!*"

With those words he left the room.

CHAPTER XV.

A Woman's Remorse.

HAVING warmed his feet to his own entire satisfaction, Horace turned round from the fireplace, and discovered that he and Lady Janet were alone.

"Can I see Grace?" he asked.

The easy tone in which he put the question—a tone, as it were, of proprietorship in "Grace"—jarred on Lady Janet at the moment. For the first time in her life she found herself comparing Horace with Julian to Horace's disadvantage. He was rich; he was a gentleman of ancient lineage; he bore an unblemished character. But who had the strong brain? who had the great heart? Which was the Man of the two?

"Nobody can see her," answered Lady Janet. "Not even you!"

The tone of the reply was sharp—with a dash of irony in it. But where is the modern young man—possessed of health and an independent income—who is capable of understanding that irony can be pre-

sumptuous enough to address itself to *him?* Horace
(with perfect politeness) declined to consider himself
answered.

"Does your ladyship mean that Miss Roseberry is
in bed?" he asked.

"I mean that Miss Roseberry is in her room. I
mean that I have twice tried to persuade Miss Roseberry to dress and come downstairs—and tried in
vain. I mean that what Miss Roseberry refuses to do
for Me, she is not likely to do for You——"

How many more meanings of her own Lady Janet
might have gone on enumerating, it is not easy to
calculate. At her third sentence, a sound in the
library caught her ear through the incompletely-closed
door, and suspended the next words on her lips.
Horace heard it also. It was the rustling sound
(travelling nearer and nearer over the library carpet)
of a silken dress.

(In the interval while a coming event remains in
a state of uncertainty, what is it the inevitable tendency of every Englishman under thirty to do? His
inevitable tendency is to ask somebody to bet on the
event. He can no more resist it than he can resist
lifting his stick or his umbrella, in the absence of a

gun, and pretending to shoot if a bird flies by him while he is out for a walk.)

"What will your ladyship bet that this is not Grace?" cried Horace.

Her ladyship took no notice of the proposal; her attention remained fixed on the library door. The rustling sound stopped for a moment. The door was softly pushed open. The false Grace Roseberry entered the room.

Horace advanced to meet her, opened his lips to speak, and stopped—struck dumb by the change in his affianced wife since he had seen her last. Some terrible oppression seemed to have crushed her. It was as if she had actually shrunk in height as well as in substance. She walked more slowly than usual; she spoke more rarely than usual, and in a lower tone. To those who had seen her before the fatal visit of the stranger from Mannheim, it was the wreck of the woman that now appeared, instead of the woman herself. And yet, there was the old charm still surviving through it all; the grandeur of the head and eyes, the delicate symmetry of the features, the unsought grace of every movement—in a word, the unconquerable beauty which suffering cannot destroy, and which time itself is powerless to wear out.

Lady Janet advanced, and took her with hearty kindness by both hands.

"My dear child, welcome among us again! You have come downstairs to please me?"

She bent her head in silent acknowledgment that it was so. Lady Janet pointed to Horace: "Here is somebody who has been longing to see you, Grace."

She never looked up; she stood submissive, her eyes fixed on a little basket of coloured wools which hung on her arm. "Thank you, Lady Janet," she said, faintly. "Thank you, Horace."

Horace placed her arm in his, and led her to the sofa. She shivered as she took her seat, and looked round her. It was the first time she had seen the dining-room since the day when she had found herself face to face with the dead-alive.

"Why do you come here, my love?" asked Lady Janet. "The drawing-room would have been a warmer and a pleasanter place for you."

"I saw a carriage at the front door. I was afraid of meeting with visitors in the drawing-room."

As she made that reply, the servant came in, and

announced the visitor's names. Lady Janet sighed
wearily. "I must go and get rid of them," she said,
resigning herself to circumstances. "What will *you*
do, Grace?"

"I will stay here, if you please."

"I will keep her company," added Horace.

Lady Janet hesitated. She had promised to see
her nephew in the dining-room on his return to the
house—and to see him alone. Would there be time
enough to get rid of the visitors and to establish her
adopted daughter in the empty drawing-room, before
Julian appeared? It was a ten minutes' walk to the
lodge, and he had to make the gatekeeper understand
his instructions. Lady Janet decided that she had
time enough at her disposal. She nodded kindly to
Mercy, and left her alone with her lover.

Horace seated himself in the vacant place on the
sofa. So far as it was in his nature to devote himself
to any one, he was devoted to Mercy. "I am grieved
to see how you have suffered," he said, with honest
distress in his face as he looked at her. "Try to
forget what has happened."

"I am trying to forget. Do *you* think of it much?"

"My darling, it is too contemptible to be thought of."

She placed her work basket on her lap. Her wasted fingers began absently sorting the wools inside.

"Have you seen Mr. Julian Gray?" she asked suddenly.

"Yes."

"What does *he* say about it?" She looked at Horace for the first time, steadily scrutinising his face. Horace took refuge in prevarication.

"I really haven't asked for Julian's opinion," he said.

She looked down again, with a sigh, at the basket on her lap—considered a little—and tried him once more.

"Why has Mr. Julian Gray not been here for a whole week?" she went on. "The servants say he has been abroad. Is that true?"

It was useless to deny it. Horace admitted that the servants were right.

Her fingers suddenly stopped at their restless work among the wools: her breath quickened perceptibly. What had Julian Gray been doing abroad? Had he been making inquiries? Did he alone, of all the people who saw that terrible meeting, suspect

her? Yes! His was the finer intelligence; his was a
clergyman's (a London clergyman's) experience of
frauds and deceptions, and of the women who were
guilty of them. Not a doubt of it now! Julian suspected her.

"When does he come back?" she asked, in tones
so low that Horace could barely hear her.

"He has come back already. He returned last
night."

A faint shade of colour stole slowly over the
pallor of her face. She suddenly put her basket away,
and clasped her hands together to quiet the trembling
of them, before she asked her next question.

"Where is"——— She paused to steady her voice.
"Where is the person," she resumed, "who came here
and frightened me?"

Horace hastened to reassure her. "The person
will not come again," he said. "Don't talk of her!
Don't think of her!"

She shook her head. "There is something I want
to know," she persisted. "How did Mr. Julian Gray
become acquainted with her?"

This was easily answered. Horace mentioned the
consul at Mannheim, and the letter of introduction.

She listened eagerly, and said her next words in a louder, firmer tone.

"She was quite a stranger, then, to Mr. Julian Gray —before that?"

"Quite a stranger," Horace replied. "No more questions—not another word about her, Grace! I forbid the subject. Come, my own love!" he said, taking her hand, and bending over her tenderly, "rally your spirits! We are young—we love each other— now is our time to be happy!"

Her hand turned suddenly cold, and trembled in his. Her head sank with a helpless weariness on her breast. Horace rose in alarm.

"You are cold—you are faint," he said. "Let me get you a glass of wine!—let me mend the fire!"

The decanters were still on the luncheon-table. Horace insisted on her drinking some port wine. She barely took half the contents of the wine-glass. Even that little told on her sensitive organisation; it roused her sinking energies of body and mind. After watching her anxiously, without attracting her notice, Horace left her again to attend to the fire at the other end of the room. Her eyes followed him slowly with a hard and tearless despair. "Rally your spirits," she repeated to herself in a whisper. "My spirits! Oh, God!" She looked round her at the luxury and beauty of the room, as those look who take their leave of familiar scenes. The moment after, her eyes sank, and rested on the rich dress that she wore—a gift from Lady Janet. She thought of the past; she thought of the future. Was the time near when she would be back again in the Refuge, or back again in the streets?—she who had been Lady Janet's adopted daughter, and Horace Holmcroft's betrothed wife! A sudden frenzy of recklessness seized on her as she thought of the coming end. Horace was right! Why not rally her spirits? Why not make the most of her time? The last hours of her life in that house were at hand. Why not enjoy her stolen position while she could? "Adventuress!" whispered the mocking spirit within her, "be true to your character. Away with your remorse! Remorse is the luxury of an honest woman." She caught up her basket of wools, inspired by a new idea. "Ring the bell!" she cried out to Horace at the fire-place.

He looked round in wonder. The sound of her voice was so completely altered that he almost fancied there must have been another woman in the room.

"Ring the bell!" she repeated. "I have left my work upstairs. If you want me to be in good spirits, I must have my work."

Still looking at her, Horace put his hand mechanically to the bell and rang. One of the men-servants came in.

"Go upstairs, and ask my maid for my work," she said sharply. Even the man was taken by surprise; it was her habit to speak to the servants with a gentleness and consideration which had long since won all their hearts. "Do you hear me?" she asked impatiently. The servant bowed, and went out on his errand. She turned to Horace with flashing eyes and fevered cheeks.

"What a comfort it is," she said, "to belong to the upper classes! A poor woman has no maid to dress her, and no footman to send upstairs. Is life worth having, Horace, on less than five thousand a year!"

The servant returned with a strip of embroidery. She took it with an insolent grace, and told him to bring her a footstool. The man obeyed. She tossed the embroidery away from her on the sofa. "On second thoughts I don't care about my work," she said. "Take it upstairs again." The perfectly-trained servant, marvelling privately, obeyed once more. Horace, in silent astonishment, advanced to the sofa to observe her more nearly. "How grave you look!" she exclaimed, with an air of flippant unconcern. "You don't approve of my sitting idle, perhaps? Anything to please you! *I* haven't got to go up and down stairs. Ring the bell again."

"My dear Grace," Horace remonstrated gravely, "you are quite mistaken. I never even thought of your work."

"Never mind; it's inconsistent to send for my work, and then send it away again. Ring the bell."

Horace looked at her, without moving. "Grace!" he said, "what has come to you?"

"How should I know?" she retorted carelessly. "Didn't you tell me to rally my spirits? Will you ring the bell? or must I?"

Horace submitted. He frowned as he walked back to the bell. He was one of the many people who instinctively resent anything that is new to them. This strange outbreak was quite new to him. For the first time in his life he felt sympathy for a servant, when the much-enduring man appeared once more.

"Bring my work back; I have changed my mind." With that brief explanation she reclined luxuriously on the soft sofa cushions; swinging one of her balls of wool to and fro above her head, and looking at it lazily as she lay back. "I have a remark to make, Horace," she went on, when the door had closed on her messenger. "It is only people in our rank of life who get good servants. Did you notice? Nothing upsets that man's temper. A servant in a poor family would have been impudent; a maid-of-all-work would have wondered when I was going to know my own mind." The man returned with the embroidery. This time she received him graciously; she dismissed him with her thanks. "Have you seen your mother lately, Horace?" she asked, suddenly sitting up and busying herself with her work.

"I saw her yesterday," Horace answered.

"She understands, I hope, that I am not well enough to call on her? She is not offended with me?"

Horace recovered his serenity. The deference to his mother implied in Mercy's questions gently flattered his self-esteem. He resumed his place on the sofa.

"Offended with you!" he answered, smiling. "My

dear Grace, she sends you her love. And, more than
that, she has a wedding-present for you."

Mercy became absorbed in her work; she stooped
close over the embroidery—so close that Horace could
not see her face. "Do you know what the present
is?" she asked in lower tones; speaking absently.

"No. I only know it is waiting for you. Shall I
go and get it to-day?"

She neither accepted nor refused the proposal—
she went on with her work more industriously than
ever.

"There is plenty of time," Horace persisted. "I
can go before dinner."

Still she took no notice: still she never looked up.
"Your mother is very kind to me," she said, abruptly.
"I was afraid at one time that she would think me
hardly good enough to be your wife."

Horace laughed indulgently: his self-esteem was
more gently flattered than ever.

"Absurd!" he exclaimed. "My darling, you are
connected with Lady Janet Roy. Your family is almost as good as ours."

"Almost?" she repeated. "Only almost?"

The momentary levity of expression vanished from

Horace's face. The family-question was far too serious a question to be lightly treated. A becoming shadow of solemnity stole over his manner. He looked as if it was Sunday, and he was just stepping into church.

"In OUR family," he said, "we trace back—by my father, to the Saxons: by my mother, to the Normans. Lady Janet's family is an old family—on her side only."

Mercy dropped her embroidery, and looked Horace full in the face. She, too, attached no common importance to what she had next to say.

"If I had not been connected with Lady Janet," she began, "would you ever have thought of marrying me?"

"My love! what is the use of asking? You *are* connected with Lady Janet."

She refused to let him escape answering her in that way.

"Suppose I had *not* been connected with Lady Janet," she persisted, "suppose I had only been a good girl, with nothing but my own merits to speak for me. What would your mother have said, then?"

Horace still parried the question—only to find the point of it pressed home on him once more.

"Why do you ask?" he said.

"I ask to be answered," she rejoined. "Would your mother have liked you to marry a poor girl, of no family—with nothing but her own virtues to speak for her?"

Horace was fairly pressed back to the wall.

"If you must know," he replied, "my mother would have refused to sanction such a marriage as that."

"No matter how good the girl might have been?"

There was something defiant—almost threatening —in her tone. Horace was annoyed, and he showed it when he spoke.

"My mother would have respected the girl, without ceasing to respect herself," he said. "My mother would have remembered what was due to the family name."

"And she would have said, No?"

"She would have said, No."

"Ah!"

There was an undertone of angry contempt in the

exclamation which made Horace start. "What is the matter?" he asked.

"Nothing," she answered, and took up her embroidery again. There he sat at her side, anxiously looking at her—his hope in the future centred in his marriage! In a week more, if she chose, she might enter that ancient family of which he had spoken so proudly, as his wife. "Oh!" she thought, "if I didn't love him! if I had only his merciless mother to think of!"

Uneasily conscious of some estrangement between them, Horace spoke again. "Surely I have not offended you?" he said.

She turned towards him once more. The work dropped unheeded on her lap. Her grand eyes softened into tenderness. A smile trembled sadly on her delicate lips. She laid one hand caressingly on his shoulder. All the beauty of her voice lent its charm to the next words that she said to him. The woman's heart hungered in its misery for the comfort that could only come from his lips.

"*You* would have loved me, Horace—without stopping to think of the family name?"

The family name again! How strangely she per-

sisted in coming back to that! Horace looked at her
without answering; trying vainly to fathom what was
passing in her mind.

She took his hand, and wrung it hard—as if she
would wring the answer out of him in that way.

"*You* would have loved me?" she repeated.

The double spell of her voice and her touch was
on him. He answered warmly, "Under any circumstances! under any name!"

She put one arm round his neck, and fixed her
eyes on his. "Is that true?" she asked.

"True as the heaven above us!"

She drank in those few commonplace words with
a greedy delight. She forced him to repeat them in
a new form.

"No matter who I might have been! For myself
alone?"

"For yourself alone."

. She threw both arms round him, and laid her
head passionately on his breast. "I love you! I love
you!! I love you!!!" Her voice rose with hysterical
vehemence at each repetition of the words—then suddenly sank to a low wailing cry of rage and despair.
The sense of her true position towards him revealed

itself in all its horror as the confession of her love escaped her lips. Her arms dropped from him; she flung herself back on the sofa cushions, hiding her face in her hands. "Oh, leave me!" she moaned faintly, "Go! go!"

Horace tried to wind his arm round her, and raise her. She started to her feet, and waved him back from her with a wild action of her hands, as if she was frightened of him. "The wedding present!" she cried, seizing the first pretext that occurred to her. "You offered to bring me your mother's present. I am dying to see what it is. Go, and get it!"

Horace tried to compose her. He might as well have tried to compose the winds and the sea.

"Go!" she repeated, pressing one clenched hand on her bosom. I am not well. Talking excites me— I am hysterical; I shall be better alone. Get me the present. Go!"

"Shall I send Lady Janet? Shall I ring for your maid?"

"Send for nobody! ring for nobody! If you love me—leave me here by myself! leave me instantly!"

"I shall see you when I come back?"

"Yes! yes!"

There was no alternative but to obey her. Unwillingly and forebodingly Horace left the room.

She drew a deep breath of relief, and dropped into the nearest chair. If Horace had stayed a moment longer—she felt it, she knew it—her head would have given way; she would have burst out before him with the terrible truth. "Oh!" she thought, pressing her cold hands on her burning eyes, "if I could only cry, now there is nobody to see me!"

The room was empty, she had every reason for concluding that she was alone. And yet, at that very moment, there were ears that listened, there were eyes waiting to see her.

Little by little the door behind her which faced the library and led into the billiard-room was opened noiselessly from without, by an inch at a time. As the opening was enlarged, a hand in a black glove, an arm in a black sleeve, appeared, guiding the movement of the door. An interval of a moment passed, and the worn white face of Grace Roseberry showed itself stealthily, looking into the dining-room.

Her eyes brightened with vindictive pleasure as they discovered Mercy sitting alone at the farther end of the room. Inch by inch she opened the door more widely, took one step forward, and checked herself. A sound, just audible at the far end of the conservatory, had caught her ear.

She listened—satisfied herself that she was not mistaken—and, drawing back with a frown of displeasure, softly closed the door again, so as to hide herself from view. The sound that had disturbed her was the distant murmur of men's voices (apparently two in number) talking together in lowered tones, at the garden entrance to the conservatory.

Who were the men? and what would they do next? They might do one of two things: they might enter the drawing-room, or they might withdraw again by way of the garden. Kneeling behind the door, with her ear at the keyhole, Grace Roseberry waited the event.

CHAPTER XVI.

They meet again.

ABSORBED in herself, Mercy failed to notice the opening door or to hear the murmur of voices in the conservatory.

The one terrible necessity which had been present

to her mind at intervals for a week past, was confronting her at that moment. She owed to Grace Roseberry the tardy justice of owning the truth. The longer her confession was delayed, the more cruelly she was injuring the woman whom she had robbed of her identity—the friendless woman who had neither witnesses nor papers to produce, who was powerless to right her own wrong. Keenly as she felt this, Mercy failed nevertheless to conquer the horror that shook her when she thought of the impending avowal. Day followed day, and still she shrank from the unendurable ordeal of confession—as she was shrinking from it now!

Was it fear for herself that closed her lips?

She trembled—as any human being in her place must have trembled—at the bare idea of finding herself thrown back again on the world, which had no place in it and no hope in it for *her*. But she could have overcome that terror—she could have resigned herself to that doom.

No! it was not the fear of the confession itself, or the fear of the consequences which must follow it, that still held her silent. The horror that daunted her was the horror of owning to Horace and to

Lady Janet that she had cheated them out of their love.

Every day, Lady Janet was kinder and kinder. Every day, Horace was fonder and fonder of her. How could she confess to Lady Janet? how could she own to Horace that she had imposed upon him? "I can't do it. They are so good to me—I can't do it!" In that hopeless way it had ended during the seven days that had gone by. In that hopeless way it ended again now.

The murmur of the two voices at the further end of the conservatory ceased. The billiard-room door opened again slowly by an inch at a time.

Mercy still kept her place, unconscious of the events that were passing round her. Sinking under the hard stress laid on it, her mind had drifted little by little into a new train of thought. For the first time, she found the courage to question the future in a new way. Supposing her confession to have been made, or supposing the woman whom she had personated to have discovered the means of exposing the fraud, what advantage, she now asked herself, would Miss Roseberry derive from Mercy Merrick's disgrace?

Could Lady Janet transfer to the woman who was really her relative by marriage the affection which she had given to the woman who had pretended to be her relative? No! All the right in the world would not put the true Grace into the false Grace's vacant place. The qualities by which Mercy had won Lady Janet's love were the qualities which were Mercy's own. Lady Janet could do rigid justice—but hers was not the heart to give itself to a stranger (and to give itself unreservedly) a second time. Grace Roseberry would be formally acknowledged—and there it would end.

Was there hope in this new view?

Yes! There was the false hope of making the inevitable atonement by some other means than by the confession of the fraud.

What had Grace Roseberry actually lost by the wrong done to her? She had lost the salary of Lady Janet's "companion and reader." Say that she wanted money, Mercy had her savings from the generous allowance made to her by Lady Janet; Mercy could offer money. Or say that she wanted employment, Mercy's interest with Lady Janet could offer employment, could offer anything Grace might ask for, if she would only come to terms.

Invigorated by the new hope, Mercy rose excitedly, weary of inaction in the empty room. She, who but a few minutes since had shuddered at the thought of their meeting again, was now eager to devise a means of finding her way privately to an interview with Grace. It should be done without loss of time—on that very day, if possible; by the next day at latest. She looked round her mechanically, pondering how to reach the end in view. Her eyes rested by chance on the door of the billiard-room.

Was it fancy? or did she really see the door first open a little—then suddenly and softly close again?

Was it fancy? or did she really hear, at the same moment, a sound behind her as of persons speaking in the conservatory?

She paused, and, looking back in that direction, listened intently. The sound—if she had really heard it—was no longer audible. She advanced towards the billiard-room, to set her first doubt at rest. She stretched out her hand to open the door—when the voices (recognisable now as the voices of two men) caught her ear once more.

This time, she was able to distinguish the words that were spoken.

"Any further orders, sir?" inquired one of the men.

"Nothing more," replied the other.

Mercy started, and faintly flushed, as the second voice answered the first. She stood irresolute close to the billiard-room, hesitating what to do next.

After an interval, the second voice made itself heard again, advancing nearer to the dining-room; "Are you there, aunt?" it asked, cautiously. There was a moment's pause. Then the voice spoke for the third time, sounding louder and nearer. "Are you there?" it reiterated; "I have something to tell you." Mercy summoned her resolution, and answered, "Lady Janet is not here." She turned, as she spoke, towards the conservatory door, and confronted on the threshold Julian Gray.

They looked at one another without exchanging a word on either side. The situation—for widely different reasons—was equally embarrassing to both of them.

There—as Julian saw *her*—was the woman forbidden to him, the woman whom he loved.

There—as Mercy saw *him*—was the man whom

she dreaded; the man whose actions (as she interpreted them) proved that he suspected her.

On the surface of it, the incidents which had marked their first meeting were now exactly repeated, with the one difference, that the impulse to withdraw, this time, appeared to be on the man's side, and not on the woman's. It was Mercy who spoke first.

"Did you expect to find Lady Janet here?" she asked, constrainedly.

He answered, on his part, more constrainedly still.

"It doesn't matter," he said. "Another time will do." ·

He drew back as he made the reply. She advanced desperately, with the deliberate intention of detaining him by speaking again.

The attempt which he had made to withdraw, the constraint in his manner when he had answered, had instantly confirmed her in the false conviction that he and he alone, had guessed the truth! If she was right —if he had secretly made discoveries abroad which placed her entirely at his mercy—the attempt to induce Grace to consent to a compromise with her would be manifestly useless. Her first and foremost interest now, was to find out how she really stood in the estimation of Julian Gray. In a terror of suspense that turned her cold from head to foot, she stopped him on his way out, and spoke to him with the piteous counterfeit of a smile.

"Lady Janet is receiving some visitors," she said. "If you will wait here, she will be back directly."

The effort of hiding her agitation from him had brought a passing colour into her cheeks. Worn and wasted as she was, the spell of her beauty was strong enough to hold him against his own will. All he had to tell Lady Janet was that he had met one of the gardeners in the conservatory, and had cautioned him as well as the lodge-keeper. It would have been easy to write this, and to send the note to his aunt on quitting the house. For the sake of his own peace of mind, for the sake of his duty to Horace, he was doubly bound to make the first polite excuse that occurred to him, and to leave Mercy as he had found her, alone in the room. He made the attempt, and hesitated. Despising himself for doing it, he allowed himself to look at her. Their eyes met. Julian stepped into the dining-room.

"If I am not in the way," he said, confusedly, "I will wait, as you kindly propose."

She noticed his embarrassment; she saw that he was strongly restraining himself from looking at her again. Her own eyes dropped to the ground as she made the discovery. Her speech failed her; her heart throbbed faster and faster.

"If I look at him again" (was the thought in *her* mind) "I shall fall at his feet and tell him all that I have done!"

"If I look at her again" (was the thought in *his* mind) "I shall fall at her feet and own that I am in love with her!"

With downcast eyes he placed a chair for her. With downcast eyes she bowed to him and took it. A dead silence followed. Never was any human misunderstanding more intricately complete than the misunderstanding which had now established itself between these two!

Mercy's work-basket was near her. She took it, and gained time for composing herself by pretending to arrange the coloured wools. He stood behind her chair, looking at the graceful turn of her head, looking at the rich masses of her hair. He reviled himself as the weakest of men, as the falsest of friends, for still remaining near her—and yet he remained.

The silence continued. The billiard-room door opened again noiselessly. The face of the listening woman appeared stealthily behind it.

At the same moment Mercy roused herself and spoke: "Won't you sit down?" she said, softly; still not looking round at him; still busy with her basket of wools.

He turned to get a chair—turned so quickly that he saw the billiard-room door move, as Grace Roseberry closed it again.

"Is there any one in that room?" he asked, addressing Mercy.

"I don't know," she answered. "I thought I saw the door open and shut again a little while ago."

He advanced at once to look into the room. As he did so, Mercy dropped one of her balls of wool. He stopped to pick it up for her—then threw open the door and looked into the billiard-room. It was empty.

Had some person been listening, and had that person retreated in time to escape discovery? The open door of the smoking-room showed that room also to be empty. A third door was open—the door of the side-hall, leading into the grounds. After a moment's consideration Julian closed it, and returned to the dining-room.

"I can only suppose," he said to Mercy, "that the billiard-room door was not properly shut, and that the draught of air from the hall must have moved it."

She accepted the explanation in silence. He was, to all appearance, not quite satisfied with it himself. For a moment or two he looked about him uneasily. Then the old fascination fastened its hold on him again. Once more he looked at the graceful turn of her head, at the rich masses of her hair. The courage to put the critical question to him, now that she had lured him into remaining in the room, was still a courage that failed her. She remained as busy as ever with her work—too busy to look at him; too busy to speak to him. The silence became unendurable. He broke it by making a commonplace inquiry after her health.

"I am well enough to be ashamed of the anxiety I have caused and the trouble I have given," she answered. "To-day I have got downstairs for the first time. I am trying to do a little work." She looked

into the basket. The various specimens of wool in
it were partly in balls and partly in loose skeins. The
skeins were mixed and tangled. "Here is sad confusion!" she exclaimed timidly, with a faint smile.
"How am I to set it right again?"

"Let me help you," said Julian.

"You!"

"Why not?" he asked, with a momentary return
of the quaint humour which she remembered so well.
"You forget that I am a curate. Curates are privileged to make themselves useful to young ladies. Let
me try."

He took a stool at her feet, and set himself to
unravel one of the tangled skeins. In a minute the
wool was stretched on his hands, and the loose end
was ready for Mercy to wind. There was something
in the trivial action, and in the homely attention that
it implied, which in some degree quieted her fear of
him. She began to roll the wool off his hands into a
ball. Thus occupied, she said the daring words which
were to lead him little by little into betraying his suspicions, if he did indeed suspect the truth.

CHAPTER XVII.

The Guardian Angel.

"You were here when I fainted, were you not?" Mercy began. "You must think me a sad coward, even for a woman."

He shook his head. "I am far from thinking that," he replied. "No courage could have sustained the shock which fell on you. I don't wonder that you fainted. I don't wonder that you have been ill."

She paused in rolling up the ball of wool. What did those words of unexpected sympathy mean? Was he laying a trap for her? Urged by that serious doubt, she questioned him more boldly.

"Horace tells me you have been abroad," she said. "Did you enjoy your holiday?"

"It was no holiday. I went abroad because I thought it right to make certain inquiries"—— He stopped there, unwilling to return to a subject that was painful to her.

Her voice sank, her fingers trembled round the ball of wool—but she managed to go on.

"Did you arrive at any results?" she asked.

"At no results worth mentioning."

The caution of that reply renewed her worst suspicions of him. In sheer despair, she spoke out plainly.

"I want to know your opinion"—— she began.

"Gently!" said Julian. "You are entangling the wool again."

"I want to know your opinion of the person who so terribly frightened me. Do you think her"——

"Do I think her—what?"

"Do you think her an adventuress?"

(As she said those words the branches of a shrub in the conservatory were noiselessly parted by a hand in a black glove. The face of Grace Roseberry appeared dimly behind the leaves. Undiscovered, she had escaped from the billiard-room, and had stolen her way into the conservatory as the safer hiding place of the two. Behind the shrub she could see as well as listen. Behind the shrub she waited, as patiently as ever.)

"I take a more merciful view," Julian answered. "I believe she is acting under a delusion. I don't blame her: I pity her."

"You pity her!" As Mercy repeated the words,

she took from Julian's hands the last lengths of wool left, and threw the imperfectly-wound skein back into the basket. "Does that mean," she resumed abruptly, "that you believe her?"

Julian rose from his seat, and looked at Mercy in astonishment.

"Good heavens, Miss Roseberry! what put such an idea as that into your head?"

"I am little better than a stranger to you," she rejoined, with an effort to assume a jesting tone. "You met that person before you met with me. It is not so very far from pitying her to believing her. How could I feel sure that you might not suspect me?"

"Suspect *you!*" he exclaimed. "You don't know how you distress, how you shock me. Suspect *you!* The bare idea of it never entered my mind. The man doesn't live who trusts you more implicitly, who believes in you more devotedly than I do."

His eyes, his voice, his manner, all told her that those words came from the heart. She contrasted his generous confidence in her (the confidence of which she was unworthy) with her ungracious distrust of him. Not only had she wronged Grace Roseberry—she had wronged Julian Gray. Could she deceive *him*

17*

as she had deceived the others? Could she meanly accept that implicit trust, that devoted belief? Never had she felt the base submissions which her own imposture condemned her to undergo, with a loathing of them so overwhelming as the loathing that she felt now. In horror of herself, she turned her head aside in silence, and shrank from meeting his eye. He noticed the movement, placing his own interpretation on it. Advancing closer, he asked anxiously if he had offended her?

"You don't know how your confidence touches me," she said, without looking up. "You little think how keenly I feel your kindness."

She checked herself abruptly. Her fine tact warned her that she was speaking too warmly—that the expression of her gratitude might strike him as being strangely exaggerated. She handed him her work-basket, before he could speak again.

"Will you put it away for me?" she asked in her quieter tones. "I don't feel able to work just now."

His back was turned on her for a moment, while he placed the basket on a side table. In that moment, her mind advanced at a bound from present to future. Accident might one day put the true Grace in possession of the proofs that she needed, and might reveal the false Grace to him in the identity that was her own. What would he think of her then? Could she make him tell her, without betraying herself? She determined to try.

"Children are notoriously insatiable if you once answer their questions, and women are nearly as bad," she said, when Julian returned to her. "Will your patience hold out if I go back for the third time to the person whom we have been speaking of?"

"Try me," he answered with a smile.

"Suppose you had *not* taken your merciful view of her?"

"Yes?"

"Suppose you believed that she was wickedly bent on deceiving others for a purpose of her own—would you not shrink from such a woman in horror and disgust?"

"God forbid that I should shrink from any human creature!" he answered earnestly. "Who among us has a right to do that?"

She hardly dared trust herself to believe him. "You would still pity her?" she persisted, "and still feel for her?"

"With all my heart."

"Oh, how good you are!"

He held up his hand in warning. The tones of his voice deepened; the lustre of his eyes brightened. She had stirred in the depths of that great heart the faith in which the man lived—the steady principle which guided his modest and noble life.

"No!" he cried. "Don't say that! Say that I try to love my neighbour as myself. Who but a Pharisee can believe he is better than another? The best among us to-day may, but for the mercy of God, be the worst among us to-morrow. The true Christian virtue is the virtue which never despairs of a fellow-creature. The true Christian faith believes in Man as well as in God. Frail and fallen as we are, we can rise on the wings of repentance from earth to heaven. Humanity is sacred. Humanity has its immortal destiny. Who shall dare say to man or woman, 'There is no hope in you?' Who shall dare say the work is all vile, when that work bears on it the stamp of the Creator's hand?"

He turned away for a moment, struggling with the emotion which she had roused in him.

Her eyes, as they followed him, lighted with a momentary enthusiasm—then sank wearily in the vain regret which comes too late. Ah! if he could have been her friend and her adviser on the fatal day when she first turned her steps towards Mablethorpe House! She sighed bitterly as the hopeless aspiration wrung her heart. He heard the sigh; and, turning again, looked at her with a new interest in his face.

"Miss Roseberry," he said.

She was still absorbed in the bitter memories of the past: she failed to hear him.

"Miss Roseberry," he repeated, approaching her.

She looked up at him with a start.

"May I venture to ask you something?" he said gently.

She shrank at the question.

"Don't suppose I am speaking out of mere curiosity," he went on. "And pray don't answer me, unless you can answer without betraying any confidence which may have been placed in you."

"Confidence!" she repeated. "What confidence do you mean?"

"It has just struck me that you might have felt more than a common interest in the questions which you put to me a moment since," he answered. "Were you by any chance speaking of some unhappy woman

—not the person who frightened you, of course—but of some other woman whom you know?"

Her head sank slowly on her bosom. He had plainly no suspicion that she had been speaking of herself: his tone and manner both answered for it that his belief in her was as strong as ever. Still, those last words made her tremble; she could not trust herself to reply to them.

He accepted the bending of her head as a reply.

"Are you interested in her?" he asked next.

She faintly answered this time. "Yes."

"Have you encouraged her?"

"I have not dared to encourage her."

His face lit up suddenly with enthusiasm. "Go to her," he said, "and let me go with you and help you!"

The answer came faintly and mournfully. "She has sunk too low for that!"

He interrupted her with a gesture of impatience.

"What has she done?" he asked.

"She has deceived—basely deceived—innocent people who trusted her. She has wronged—cruelly wronged—another woman."

For the first time, Julian seated himself at her side. The interest that was now roused in him was an interest above reproach. He could speak to Mercy without restraint; he could look at Mercy with a pure heart.

"You judge her very harshly," he said. "Do *you* know how she may have been tried and tempted?"

There was no answer.

"Tell me," he went on, "is the person whom she has injured still living?"

"Yes."

"If the person is still living, she may atone for the wrong. The time may come when this sinner, too, may win our pardon and deserve our respect."

"Could *you* respect her?" Mercy asked, sadly. "Can such a mind as yours understand what she has gone through?"

A smile, kind and momentary, brightened his attentive face.

"You forget my melancholy experience," he answered. "Young as I am, I have seen more than most men of women who have sinned and suffered. Even after the little that you have told me, I think I can put myself in her place. I can well understand, for instance, that she may have been tempted beyond human resistance. Am I right?"

"You are right."

"She may have had nobody near at the time to advise her, to warn her, to save her. Is that true?"

"It is true."

"Tempted and friendless, self-abandoned to the evil impulse of the moment, this woman may have committed herself headlong to the act which she now vainly repents. She may long to make atonement, and may not know how to begin. All her energies may be crushed under the despair and horror of herself, out of which the truest repentance grows. Is such a woman as this all wicked, all vile? I deny it! She may have a noble nature; and she may show it nobly yet. Give her the opportunity she needs—and our poor fallen fellow-creature may take her place again among the best of us; honoured, blameless, happy once more!"

Mercy's eyes, resting eagerly on him while he was speaking, dropped again despondingly when he had done.

"There is no such future as that," she answered, "for the woman whom I am thinking of. She has lost her opportunity. She has done with hope."

Julian gravely considered with himself for a moment.

"Let us understand each other," he said. "She has

committed an act of deception to the injury of another woman. Was that what you told me?"

"Yes."

"And she has gained something to her own advantage by the act?"

"Yes."

"Is she threatened with discovery?"

"She is safe from discovery—for the present, at least."

"Safe as long as she closes her lips?"

"As long as she closes her lips."

"There is her opportunity!" cried Julian. "Her future is before her. She has *not* done with hope."

With clasped hands, in breathless suspense, Mercy looked at that inspiriting face, and listened to those golden words.

"Explain yourself," she said. "Tell her, through me, what she must do."

"Let her own the truth," answered Julian, "without the base fear of discovery to drive her to it. Let her do justice to the woman whom she has wronged, while that woman is still powerless to expose her. Let her sacrifice everything that she has gained by the fraud to the sacred duty of atonement. If she can do that

—for conscience sake and for pity's sake—to her own
prejudice, to her own shame, to her own loss—then
her repentance has nobly revealed the noble nature
that is in her; then she is a woman to be trusted, respected, beloved! If I saw the Pharisees and Fanatics
of this lower earth passing her by in contempt, I would
hold out my hand to her before them all. I would
say to her in her solitude and her affliction. 'Rise,
poor wounded heart! Beautiful, purified soul, God's
angels rejoice over you! Take your place among the
noblest of God's creatures!'"

In those last sentences, he unconsciously repeated
the language in which he had spoken to his outcast
congregation in the Chapel of the Refuge. With tenfold power and tenfold persuasion they now found
their way again to Mercy's heart. Softly, suddenly,
mysteriously, a change passed over her. Her troubled
face grew beautifully still. The shifting light of terror
and suspense vanished from her grand grey eyes, and
left in them the steady inner glow of a high and pure
resolve.

There was a moment of silence between them.
They both had need of silence. Julian was the first
to speak again.

"Have I satisfied you that her opportunity is still before her?" he asked. "Do you feel, as I feel, that she has *not* done with hope?"

"You have satisfied me that the world holds no truer friend to her than you," Mercy answered gently and gratefully. "She shall prove herself worthy of your generous confidence in her. She shall show you yet, that you have not spoken in vain."

Still inevitably failing to understand her, he led the way to the door.

"Don't waste the precious time," he said. "Don't leave her cruelly to herself. If you can't go to her, let me go as your messenger, in your place."

She stopped him by a gesture. He took a step back into the room, and paused; observing with surprise that she made no attempt to move from the chair that she occupied.

"Stay here," she said to him in slightly-altered tones.

"Pardon me," he rejoined, "I don't understand you."

"You will understand me directly. Give me a little time."

He still lingered near the door, with his eyes fixed

inquiringly on her. A man of a lower nature than his, or a man believing in Mercy less devotedly than he believed, would now have felt his first suspicion of her. Julian was as far as ever from suspecting her, even yet.

"Do you wish to be alone?" he asked considerately. "Shall I leave you for awhile and return again?" •

She looked up with a start of terror. "Leave me?" she repeated, and suddenly checked herself on the point of saying more. Nearly half the length of the room divided them from each other. The words which she was longing to say were words that would never pass her lips, unless she could see some encouragement in his face. "No!" she cried out to him on a sudden, in her sore need, "don't leave me! Come back to me!"

He obeyed her in silence. In silence, on her side, she pointed to the chair near her. He took it. She looked at him, and checked herself again; resolute to make her terrible confession, yet still hesitating how to begin. Her woman's instinct whispered to her, "Find courage in his touch!" She said to him, simply and artlessly said to him, "Give me encouragement.

Give me strength. Let me take your hand." He neither answered nor moved. His mind seemed to have become suddenly preoccupied; his eyes rested on her vacantly; he was on the brink of discovering her secret; in another instant he would have found his way to the truth. In that instant, innocently as his sister might have taken it, she took his hand. The soft clasp of her fingers, clinging round his, roused his senses, fired his passion for her, swept out of his mind the pure aspirations which had filled it but the moment before, paralysed his perception when it was just penetrating the mystery of her disturbed manner and her strange words. All the man in him trembled under the rapture of her touch. But the thought of Horace was still present to him: his hand lay passive in hers; his eyes looked uneasily away from her.

She innocently strengthened her clasp of his hand. She innocently said to him, "Don't look away from me. Your eyes give me courage."

His hand returned the pressure of hers. He tasted to the full the delicious joy of looking at her. She had broken down his last reserves of self-control. The thought of Horace, the sense of honour, became obscured in him. In a moment more he might have

said the words which he would have depl
rest of his life, if she had not stopped hir
ing first. "I have more to say to you," :
abruptly, feeling the animating resolutior
heart bare before him at last; "more, far :
have said yet. Generous, merciful friend,
it *here!*"

She attempted to throw herself on h
his feet. He sprang from his seat and c
holding her with both his hands, raising
rose himself. In the words which had j
her, in the startling action which had a
them, the truth burst on him.

The guilty woman she had spoken of v

END OF VOL. I.

www.ingramcontent.com/pod-product-compliance
Lightning Source LLC
Chambersburg PA
CBHW030637030726
47497CB00006B/1824